LIFE CHANGING PROMISES!

BY

Dr. Harvey B. Bee

FZM Publishing

All Scriptures, unless indicated, are taken from the King James Version

Scriptures quotations marked NJKV are taken from the New King James Version

Scriptures quotations marked NIV are taken from the New International Version.

ISBN
978-0-615-25334-3

Printed in the United States of America.

TABLE OF CONTENT

FOREWORD

When I think of Dr. Harvey Bee I think of a steaming locomotive moving down the tracks ready to plow through any obstacle or crisis that may be trying to block the way.

Dr. Bee, as a father there is none greater. I've watched him with his family he is a loved and gracious dad and husband.

As a Bishop and Pastor Dr. Bee walking in the path of integrity and love, he has become the spiritual father of thousands. His mentorship and wisdom have unlocked so many in his local church.

As an author Dr. Harvey is now extending His gifts and ability to help others walk into their season of promise and blessings.

I believe this book will become the catalyst we need to propel us into our faith walk... love walk... and the walk of prosperity and blessing.

God's word is packed full of blessings. Psalm 68:19 says God loads us down daily with benefits. This means that every day God is sending to our lives miracles and blessings. The only reason some of haven't yet received them is that we are not willing to see them. Seeing decides receiving.

The difference in people is what they see...

David saw the door to his future while the children of Israel saw a giant wanting to kill them.   Dr. Bee had placed in these pages the information necessary to train us to see better... to hear better... to believe better.

This will be, in my opinion, the best read for you this year. I hope you inquired more than one copy. Give this book to all those you want to help reach their potential future.

Sincerely,

Dr. Jerry A. Grillo, Jr.
The Favor Center
P.O. Box 3707 Hickory, NC. 28603
www. Bishopgrillo.com

ACKNOWLEDGEMENTS

It is with great pleasure, esteem, gratitude, and appreciation that I thank our Lord and Savior, Jesus Christ, who blessed us to be alive and allowed us to use our gifts and talents to build His Kingdom.

Special thanks to my beautiful wife, Veronica; my lovely daughter, Mira; my handsome son, Jarius; and my awesome son, Carlos who mean more to me than I could ever express.

Thanks to my father, Bishop Wesley Bee, Jr.; my mother. Earnestine P. Bee, my father-in-law, Pastor James H. Brown, Jr., my mother-in-law, Claydes Brown; my father, Burley Adams, Jr.; my mother, Mary Adams; my late grandmother, Lizzie Mae Humphey-Philpart; late grandfather, Ardie Lee Peterson; my spiritual father, Bishop Willie L. Reid, Sr., my spiritual mother, Gloria Reid; good friends, Dr. Dave and Ann Wilcoxson; my awesome friends Apostle Dr. Cornelius and Deon Sanders, and my great friends Pastor Kenneth and Latoshia Kirksey, Sr., for being great examples of righteousness and integrity.

Thanks to my Executive Administrative Assistant, Cassandra Wrenn, my School Administrator, Dr. Yvette Brown, and my Media Journalist, Leslie Harriell-Turner, who took the time to read through all of my typing and correcting any errors I may have made.

I would also like to express thanks to my family, friends, relatives, spiritual sons in the ministry, and church family (Christian Fellowship Church) who believe that I am a Man of God! We are One People, with One Vision, and we operate under One Power (the Holy Spirit). Thank you for your commitment and love for me and my family.

A special thanks to you, the readers, for investing in yourselves. I agree with you that what God has for you—it is for you! Tap into your promises!

PREFACE

I have found out that there are many people who stroll through life without ever knowing the many promises that God has given them. I believe after reading this book you will find that there are so many promises that are yet to be discovered by you and people like you. Life is like a treasure hunt. Each day that we live, we have the opportunity to discover the treasures which God has for us, to bless our lives. As you open this book and begin to read, my prayer is that you ascertain some things about your own life which God Himself has promised to fill. Treasures uncovered, undiscovered, unexposed, concealed, hidden, unrevealed, and unseen will be brought to you face to face and eliminated in such a way that you will begin to praise God like never before! When we come to the place that we are willing to do it God's way, we will have the "promise of the life that now is, and of that which is to come." After all is said and done, one thing we know for sure is that God has promised eternal life to all who believe and receive Him. Find out what God has to say or better still what God has said about what He has promised you and your family from the beginning. I am convinced after exploring this book your life will be improved greatly! Let's begin, shall we...

Chapter One

WHO MADE THE PROMISES?

God made the promises. Many years ago, God promised me that He would heal my body and He did. He promised me that he would save my household and He did. He promised me that He would bless my ministry and He has. He promised me that he would prosper me and He has.

PROMISED TESTIMONY

As a child, I was born with asthma and the doctor said that I would never be like normal children. My father and mother shared with me early in life that God promised them that He would heal me and I believed them. Having no medical benefits and little money, we believed in the power of prayer. My momma, a praying Woman of God, always taught me to carry a bottle of olive oil with me which had been prayed over, blessed and anointed by the Elders of the Church. This bottle of anointed oil was to be opened and a finger tip dip placed on my forehead anytime I felt an attack coming. I can remember at the young tender age of nine, battling an asthma attack at Lella-Ellis Elementary School. We were playing in the water tunnels which had no water in them at that time; these tunnels were large enough to crawl in or walk (bending over) through. As we were playing, dust begins to fly up in the tunnel and I could feel the dust as it hit my nostrils. Before I knew anything, I was breathing hard and experiencing shortness of breath. All I could think of was my mother telling me to anoint myself with the bottle of oil located in the right front pocket of my jeans. As I reached down into the pocket of my dusty black jeans, I located the thing that changed my life forever! I anointed myself for the last time for Asthma! Immediately as I anointed myself, and prayed I felt the Holy Spirit (of course, I didn't know fully what it was at that time) anoint me and I was healed that day! All because of a promise God made in His Word for me years ago, the course of my life was changed. The Lord is *Jehovah-Rapha*; the Lord that healeth. The Word of God says, I am the Lord your health! I'm here today as a living miracle and a walking testimony of what God can and will do. Why? Because He promised to heal me! This promise changed my life and it can change yours as well!

In 1987, my wife and I had the pleasure of meeting Bishop and First Lady Phillip Porter of All Nations Church of God in Christ in Aurora, Colorado, they had nine children. To our amazement, all nine of their children had accepted Jesus Christ as their personal Lord and Savior and were doing well in ministry. We were so impressed with the discipline, joy, and peace that we observed in each member of this family. In our minds, we could not believe that a man and woman of God could have so many children who were all living saved, stress-free, loving-life just as God promises in His Word. But our hearts were turned to the scripture about Cornelius' house that said:

Acts 10:1, "At Caesarea there was a man named Cornelius, a centurion in what was known as the Italian Regiment." *(New International Version)*

Acts 10:2, "He and **all his family were devout and God-fearing**; he gave generously to those in need and prayed to God regularly." *(New International Version)*

God's promise to me was that He would save me and my household just as He did the Porter's house. All of my children are saved and doing well. This was done all because of God's promises.

I am blessed spiritually, financially, physically, mentally, emotionally, intellectually, naturally, supernaturally and highly favored by the Lord Jesus Christ because of His promises.

I write about these promises because down through the years, I found that the Lord remains faithful to what He has promised. Enjoy as you enter into your promises—God is sure to fulfill every one of them!

ALL THE PROMISES OF GOD ARE YES!

2 Corinthians 1:20 says, "For **all the promises of God** in him are yea, and in him Amen, unto the glory of God by us."

According to the Word of God, promises are divine assurances, pledges or guarantees made by God.

2 Corinthians 1:20 says the promises of God are "Yea" and "Amen". "Yea" means "yes".

The promises of God are not "yes" then "no". They're not "I don't know" or "Maybe so".

The promises of God are "Yes!"

Will He save you? "Yes!"

Will He heal you? "Yes!"

Will He deliver you? "Yes!"

Will He set you free? "Yes!"

Will He supply your needs? "Yes!"

Will He abundantly bless you? "Yes!"

The promises of God are "Yes" and the promises of God are "Amen." Jesus said in Revelation 1:14 that He is the Amen, the faithful and true witness, and the beginning of the creation of God.

Jesus is the Amen! Amen means "So be it." Amen means "It's already done." The promises of God are "Yes." The promises of God are "So is it." The promises of God are "It's already done." Every promise in the book is "Yea and Amen" but every promise in the book is conditional. The problem God's people have with entering the Promises of God is while God is saying "Yes, it's already done" to what we want, God's people are saying "No, I can't do it." While God is saying "Yes, It's already done" to what we need, God's people are saying "No, I won't do it" to what He needs. God is looking for someone who will say "yes" to His will and "yes" to His way. God is looking for someone to say "Yea" and "Amen" to Him. God is looking for a "Yes" man. God is looking for someone who will say "Yes, I'll go", "Yes, I'll say it", "Yes, I'll do it", "Yes, I can handle it", "Yes, I can make it happen." God is looking for some "Yes" men and "Yes" women who will say "Yea and Amen" to Him.

CHAPTER TWO
GOD KEEPS HIS PROMISES!

Have you ever had someone to make a promise and not keep it? I believe we all have experienced broken promises by people. Some promises made to us have no consequences at all if they are broken, but on the other hand, there are promises if broken, have obvious consequences.

As human beings we sometimes make mistakes and of course we suffer the consequences. We find many times that God will do mighty things with our mistakes. What do we do when we have made mistakes? We delay our promise to God and eventually we come to realize that we've been living a life on broken promises? It's to our benefit to hold fast to the promises of God!

God promises and fulfills. In the mind of God, His promises are already done before man receives them. Jeremiah quoted the Lord, "For I know the thoughts that I think toward you, saith the LORD, thoughts of peace, and not of evil, to **give you an expected end**." The promises were given before we got started! It was done before we began. Therefore, it will end the way it started, in the mind of

God (in His thoughts), that things would work out alright. Why? Because He promised!

Can we believe God is good when providence seems to prohibit the fulfillment of what He has promised? Abraham is the greatest example of a yes answer to that question. Look with me at Romans 4:3, "For what saith the scripture? Abraham believed God, and it was counted unto him for righteousness." You see, "Abraham believed God!" What we must understand is that Abraham's life of faith was not free from ups and downs. It was full of them just like our lives are, many of which could have been avoided if Abraham had remembered one fundamental fact: only the one who makes the promise can fulfill it.

Abraham, like many of us, was not big on waiting. He endured the long drought of Sarah's infertility. Waiting, which means, going on in a settled certainty of faith in God's faithfulness, slipped away from his consciousness from time to time.

LESSONS WE CAN LEARN FROM ABRAHAM:

1. Abraham was "impatient" and "knew" the bonds woman... which produced a son.

2. His impatience created the consequences of that which *jealousy* brings—which eventually occurred between Sarah and the slave woman. His impatience created *sadness* within himself at the thought of Sarah's desire to send Hagar and her son away. It was obvious that he did indeed love this son and certainly did not want him out of his life.

3. Much grief could have been avoided had he waited on God's promise.

Just like we do today, our impatience often creates unnecessary drama that could have been avoided had we waited. But the beauty in this is the fact that even in spite of our mess ups (in this case impatience) through repentance, God WILL redeem us from the messes we create.

Just like Abraham who was grieved over his son's departure, God still, in the midst of Abraham's "mess up," promised him that he would take care of that particular son and stayed true to His word. God kept His promise to Abraham regarding his decadents via the child he originally spoke of –ISSAC.

A key point we must remember: If God doesn't mean it; He doesn't say it.

> *Genesis 21:1-14, "And the LORD visited Sarah as he had said, and the LORD did unto Sarah as he had spoken. For Sarah conceived, and bare Abraham a son in his old age, **at the set time** of which God had spoken to him. And Abraham called the name of his son that was born unto him, whom Sarah bare to him, Isaac. And Abraham circumcised his son Isaac being eight days old, as God had commanded him. And Abraham was an hundred years old, when his son Isaac was born unto him. And Sarah said, **God hath made me to laugh,** so that all that hear will laugh with me. And she said, Who would have said unto Abraham, that Sarah should have given children suck? for I have born him a son in his old age. And the child grew,*

and was weaned: and Abraham made a great feast the same day that Isaac was weaned. And Sarah saw the son of Hagar the Egyptian, which she had born unto Abraham, mocking. Wherefore she said unto Abraham, Cast out this bondwoman and her son: for the son of this bondwoman shall not be heir with my son, even with Isaac. And the thing was very grievous in Abraham's sight because of his son. And God said unto Abraham, Let it not be grievous in thy sight because of the lad, and because of thy bondwoman; in all that Sarah hath said unto thee, hearken unto her voice; **for in Isaac shall thy seed be called.** *And also of the son of the bondwoman* **will I make a nation, because he is thy seed.** *And Abraham rose up early in the morning, and took bread, and a bottle of water, and gave it unto Hagar, putting it on her shoulder, and the child, and sent her away: and she departed, and wandered in the wilderness of Beersheba."*

AT THE SET OR APPOINTED TIME

God's *appointed time* is inevitable. It is a done deal! If He said it, it's done! God's speaking is always for an appointed time. This is always on His appropriate timetable. God is not subject to our agenda. We are subject to His. We were created to carry out the assignment placed on our lives by God. "...let God be true, but every man a liar..." (Romans 3:4) If He spoke it, He will do it!

Job experienced a lot of grief after his temptation by Satan. Somehow he managed to encourage himself. Job said in chapter 14, verse 14, "If a man die, shall he live again? All the days of my *appointed time* will I wait, till my change come." In other words, I may be going through now, but it is only a matter of time before things change! Like Job, we must have faith in the midst of things not going our way and say, "I will wait, until my change comes." What you are faced with today is not necessarily what you will be faced with tomorrow. Believe it or not! You have an appointment!

- *You have an appointment with breakthrough!*

- *You have an appointment with increase!*

- *You have an appointment with joy!*

- *You have an appointment with healing!*

- *You have an appointment with victory!*

- *You have an appointment with your destiny!*

- *You have an appointment with your deliverance!*

- *You have an appointment with your vision!*

The very thing that God promised you; the very thing that you saw yourself doing; the very thing you saw yourself becoming **IS** for *an appointed time!*

Habakkuk 2:3 declares, "For the vision is yet for *an appointed time*, but at the end it shall speak, and not lie: though it tarry, wait for it; because it will surely come, it will not tarry."

He did not say maybe it **will** come. He did not say it **might** come. He did not say **perhaps** it will come. But he said, **"It will surely come!"** In other words, you can bank on it. If He said it, the *appointed time* has been set! All we have to do is wait for it. The manifestations of the promises of God are sure to come just like He said it. If He said it, we can come right behind Him and declare what He has said. Just say it! "I have an appointment!" "I have a date with destiny!" "I have *a set time*!"

Before Sarah conceived and gave birth to Abraham in chapter 21, God had given *a set time* in chapter 17. Genesis 17:21 says, "But my covenant will I establish with Isaac, which Sarah shall bear unto thee at this *set time* in the next year."

Four chapters later, God fulfilled His Word. Can you say, "*A set time*?" A *set time* may not be our time. But at the *set time*, God will fulfill His Promise! God had made a promise to Abraham at the age of 75 and it was not fulfilled until he was a 100 years of age. I believe if we could interview Abraham today and ask him if it was worth the wait, he would tell us with certainty, "It was well worth it." Why? Because if God promised you something, you can't leave here until it is fulfilled. Abraham was a 100 years old and he was still getting around like a teenager. What a miracle! God will preserve you, keep you, protect you, heal you, and move you until the *set time* to fulfill the promise in you.

According to the Bible, Sarah had waited many years for this baby boy. When she was told she would have a child of her own, even though the word was from God, she laughed. Maybe not so much from lack of faith in what God could do, as from unbelief in what her body could be counted on to accomplish at her age.

The *set time* for Sarah was at the age of 90. Her *set time* made her laugh. I'm just wondering, will your *set time* make you laugh? If God told you to get out of your country and from your kin folk, and from your father's house and go to a place that He will show you; and that He would make you a great nation and would bless you and make your name great and you are going to be a blessing—what would you do? Knowing that you were promised to be the father of many and not yet the father of any—what would you do? The best thing to do is wait with expectation for the *set time*! Wait for the *appointed time* just like God said! Wait for the fulfillment of the promise! For it shall surely come, if you just wait for it. Your time of blessings has already been set.

DON'T STAGGER AT THE PROMISES OF GOD!

Romans 4:20-21 says, "He **staggered** not at the **promise** of God through unbelief; but was strong in faith, giving glory to God; And being fully persuaded that, what he had **promised**, he was able also to perform."

The Greek word that describes the word **stagger** is *diakrino (dee-ak-ree'-no)* which means to separate thoroughly, to withdraw from, or oppose; to doubt, be partial, or waver.

I have seen many people who have separated, withdrawn, and/or opposed the promises of God by their actions. Maybe because they could not see with the physical eye, they didn't continue in faith. Maybe because doubt crept in, they begin to waver. Remember, if God made you a promise, He will keep His promise! We are reminded and reassured by Paul who was fully persuaded and replete with assurance that God is well able to perform or fully complete what He promised. He will backup His word with action!

Like Abraham, we have been declared righteous not by our good or righteous deeds. Say this with me, "I have been declared righteous because of my faith in God and not because of my works." The greatest thing in the world to know is that one's sins are forgiven!" It brings great joy to know that we have been made or declared righteous before our Almighty God. Once we accept Christ into our lives, our sins are longer counted against us by the Lord. This is great joy and this is good news!

God's promise is given to us as a free Gift! Abraham's faith is so important to us as believers because when God told him that he would be father of many nations; he believed God. He was not the father of any but God promised that he would be the father of many. How could this be? No problem. Abraham staggered not at the promise that God made him. The Bible said "even though such a promise seemed utterly impossible, Abraham continued to believe God. And Abraham's faith did not weaken, even though he knew that he was too old to be a father at the age of one hundred and that Sarah, his wife, had never been able to have children. Abraham never wavered in believing God's promise. In fact, his faith grew stronger, and in this he brought glory to God. He was absolutely convinced that God was able to do anything He promised. And because of Abraham's faith, God declared him to be righteous. Now this wonderful truth—that God declared him to be righteous—wasn't just for Abraham's benefit. It was for us; too, assuring us that God will also declare us to be righteous if we believe in God, who brought Jesus our Lord back from the dead. He was handed over to die because of our sins, and he was raised from the dead to make us right with God." If God told you something don't waver, don't doubt, and don't move! Allow Him to work His perfect and complete work and way in your life. The promise is yours because God said so!

CHAPTER THREE

A BLESSING THAT WILL MAKE YOU LAUGH!

Have you ever had something happen to you that was so ridiculous that it made you laugh? "Hoped, but didn't expect." That might have been Sarah's motto. She believed but could not conceive of how it could be possible for her to conceive a child. In her eyes this seemed like an unrealistic promise. Yet, when it was fulfilled, she was consumed with hilarious laughter. How could this thing be?

We may emphatically say, "That's ridiculous!" As a matter of fact, Sarah said it would be so ridiculous that God would have other people laughing along with her. Isn't that awesome— receiving something so great that will make you laugh? Some may even be laughing at you but, *(he who laughs last, laughs best.)* I truly believe that God will give you something to laugh about. All we have to do is look back from where we came. It's really ridiculous the way God has blessed you!

You didn't deserve all that you have—that's ridiculous!

You didn't have the credit to get the car that you drive, but God promised—that's ridiculous!

You didn't know how you were going to pass your algebra test, but God promised if you studied—and you found out that you made one of the top grades in the class—that's ridiculous!

You didn't have any idea that you would be living in the house that you live in right now, but God promised—that's ridiculous!

All of your family members are healthy and walking in their healing when other folk are spending all their money to get well, but God promised to be your *Jehovah-Rapha*—that's ridiculous!

They laughed and you did too when God used someone to cancel your debts, but God promised—that's ridiculous!

While reading this book, you may not have experienced the things I'm speaking about right now but, remember, God promised! He is sure to do something ridiculous in your life. Others may see it as something that should not happen to you or why did that happen to you and not them, just remember, God promised!

Just like Sarah, it maybe something so far out there, so far fetched, so (you guessed it) ridiculous that it makes you laugh. Remember, "All of the promises of God are Yes!"

To man, it's ridiculous when God does something that man can't explain, but God says this is what I promised.

Psalms 84:11, "For the LORD God is a sun and shield: the LORD will give grace and glory: **no good thing will he withhold from them that walk uprightly."**

12 PROMISES EVERY BELIEVER SHOULD REMEMBER:

A promise from God is a statement we can depend on with absolute confidence. Here are 12 promises for the Christian to claim:

1. **God's presence** -- "I will never leave thee" (Hebrews 13:5)

2. **God's protection** -- "I am thy shield" (Genesis 15:1)

3. **God's power** -- "I will strengthen thee" (Isaiah 41:10)

4. **God's provision** -- "I will help thee" (Isaiah 41:10)

5. **God's leading** -- "And when He putteth forth His own sheep, He goeth before them" (John 10:4)

6. **God's purposes** -- "I know the thoughts that I think toward you, saith the Lord, thoughts of peace, and not of evil" (Jeremiah. 20:11)

7. **God's rest** -- "Come unto Me, all ye that labor and are heavy laden, and I will give you rest" (Matthew. 11:28)

8. **God's cleansing** -- "If we confess our sins, He is faithful and just to forgive us our sins, and to cleanse us from all unrighteousness" (1 John 1:9)

9. **God's goodness** -- "No good thing will He withhold from them that walk uprightly" (Psalms 84:11)

10. **God's faithfulness** -- "The Lord will not forsake His people for His great name's sake" (1 Samuel 12:22)

11. **God's guidance** -- "The meek will He guide" (Psalms 25:9)

12. **God's wise plan** -- "All things work together for good to them that love God" (Romans 8:28)

LAW OF BLESSED CONNECTION

Have you ever heard that you are either blessed or guilty by association? Well, you are either blessed or cursed by your connections. According to Genesis, the promise was given to

Abraham and his seed. Many people think that the seed was Isaac but the seed was indeed Christ.

Galatians 3:16 NLT says, "God gave the promise to Abraham and his child. And notice that it doesn't say the promise was to his children," as if it meant many descendants. But the promise was to his child—and that, of course, means Christ."

So, if the promises that he gave Abraham were for Abraham and his seed, and we are connected with Christ; that means the same blessings that were given to Abraham are given to us!

Galatians 3:29, "And if ye be Christ's, then are ye Abraham's seed, and heirs according to the promise."

So then, every promise that was made to Abraham, if I'm a child of God, it belongs to me. Right!

So, then, every place in the Bible where God makes a promise to Abraham, I have a right as an heir of God to claim and declare it for myself. That's right!

I heard Bishop Don Mears say, "It is time the heirs of God started saying, me too, God!"

Let's break down the promise:

God said:
 We can say:

I will make thee a great nation   Me too, God!

I will bless thee	Me too, God!
I will make thy name great	Me too, God!
Thou shalt be a blessing	Me too, God!
I will bless them that bless thee	Me too, God!
I will curse him that curseth thee	Me too, God!
In thee shall all...the earth be blessed	Me too, God!
I'm going to make of thee a fruitful nation	Me too, God!
I'm going to have kings come out of thee	Me too, God!
I'm going to bless you	Me too, God!
All the land thou seest, I will give it thee	Me too, God!

Isn't it easy to get excited about all the blessings that are provided for us because we are connected by covenant with God through Abraham?

We should equally get excited about the covenant and connection we make through giving our tithes and offerings. In order to receive the Abrahamic blessings we must participate in the Abraham covenant. The Abrahamic covenant of tithes and offerings connects us to the Abraham blessings. Are we still excited?

CHAPTER FOUR

PROMISES ARE CONDITIONAL!

Notice in scripture that the **"Ifs"** are conditional promises predicated upon our decisions or choices. I believe every Christian should concern themselves with the **Ifs** in the bible. Obedience to the **"Ifs"** in the Word of God follows with a promise to the doer:

Job 36:11, "**If** they obey and serve him, they shall spend their days in prosperity, and their years in pleasures."

Isaiah 1:19, "**If** ye be willing and obedient, ye shall eat the good of the land:"

Isaiah 1:20, "But **if** ye refuse and rebel, ye shall be devoured with the sword: for the mouth of the LORD hath spoken it."

Galatians 3:29, "And **if** ye be Christ's, then are ye Abraham's seed, and heirs according to the promise."

Exodus 15:26, "And said, **If** thou wilt diligently hearken to the voice of the LORD thy God, and wilt do that which is right in his sight, and wilt give ear to his commandments, and keep all his statutes, I will put none of these diseases upon thee, which I have brought upon the Egyptians: for I am the LORD that healeth thee."

Exodus 18:23, "**If** thou shalt do this thing, and God command thee so, then thou shalt be able to endure, and all this people shall also go to their place in peace."

Exodus 19:5, "Now therefore, **if** ye will obey my voice indeed, and keep my covenant, then ye shall be a peculiar treasure unto me above all people: for all the earth is mine:"

Numbers 14:8, "**If** the LORD delight in us, then he will bring us into this land, and give it us; a land which floweth with milk and honey."

Deuteronomy 19:8, "And **if** the LORD thy God enlarge thy coast, as he hath sworn unto thy fathers, and give thee all the land which he promised to give unto thy fathers;"

Deuteronomy 19:9, "**If** thou shalt keep all these commandments to do them, which I command thee this day, to love the LORD thy God, and to walk ever in his ways; then shalt thou add three cities more for thee, beside these three:"

Deuteronomy 28:1, "And it shall come to pass, **if** thou shalt hearken diligently unto the voice of the LORD thy God, to observe and to do all his commandments which I command thee this day, that the LORD thy God will set thee on high above all nations of the earth:"

Deuteronomy 28:2, "And all these blessings shall come on thee, and overtake thee, **if** thou shalt hearken unto the voice of the LORD thy God."

Deuteronomy 28:9, "The LORD shall establish thee an holy people unto himself, as he hath sworn unto thee, **if** thou shalt keep the commandments of the LORD thy God, and walk in his ways."

1 Kings 3:14, "And **if** thou wilt walk in my ways, to keep my statutes and my commandments, as thy father David did walk, then I will lengthen thy days."

1 Kings 9:4, "And **if** thou wilt walk before me, as David thy father walked, in integrity of heart, and in uprightness, to do according to all that I have commanded thee, and wilt keep my statutes and my judgments:"

2 Kings 21:8, "Neither will I make the feet of Israel move any more out of the land which I gave their fathers; only **if** they will observe to do according to all that I have commanded them, and according to all the law that my servant Moses commanded them."

1 Chronicles 22:13, "Then shalt thou prosper, **if** thou takest heed to fulfil the statutes and judgments which the LORD charged Moses with concerning Israel: be strong, and of good courage; dread not, nor be dismayed."

1 Chronicles 28:7, "Moreover I will establish his kingdom for ever, **if** he be constant to do my commandments and my judgments, as at this day."

1 Chronicles 28:9, "And thou, Solomon my son, know thou the God of thy father, and serve him with a perfect heart and with a willing mind: for the LORD searcheth all hearts, and understandeth all the imaginations of the thoughts: **if** thou seek him, he will be found of thee; but **if** thou forsake him, he will cast thee off for ever."

2 Chronicles 7:14, "**If** my people, which are called by my name, shall humble themselves, and pray, and seek my face, and turn from their wicked ways; then will I hear from heaven, and will forgive their sin, and will heal their land."

2 Chronicles 30:9, "For **if** ye turn again unto the LORD, your brethren and your children shall find compassion before them that lead them captive, so that they shall come again into this land: for the LORD your God is gracious and merciful, and will not turn away his face from you, **if** ye return unto him."

Nehemiah 1:8, "Remember, I beseech thee, the word that thou commandedst thy servant Moses, saying, **If** ye transgress, I will scatter you abroad among the nations:"

Nehemiah 1:9, "But **if** ye turn unto me, and keep my commandments, and do them; though there were of you cast out unto the uttermost part of the heaven, yet will I gather them from thence, and will bring them unto the place that I have chosen to set my name there."

Job 8:5, "**If** thou wouldest seek unto God betimes, and make thy supplication to the Almighty;"

Job 8:6, "**If** thou wert pure and upright; surely now he would awake for thee, and make the habitation of thy righteousness prosperous."

Job 22:23, "**If** thou return to the Almighty, thou shalt be built up, thou shalt put away iniquity far from thy tabernacles."

Psalms 66:18, "**If** I regard iniquity in my heart, the Lord will not hear me:"

Jeremiah 26:3, "**If** so be they will hearken, and turn every man from his evil way, that I may repent me of the evil, which I purpose to do unto them because of the evil of their doings."

Ezekiel 18:21, "But **if** the wicked will turn from all his sins that he hath committed, and keep all my statutes, and do that which is lawful and right, he shall surely live, he shall not die."

St. Matthew 6:14, "For **if** ye forgive men their trespasses, your heavenly Father will also forgive you:"

St. Matthew 6:15, "But **if** ye forgive not men their trespasses, neither will your Father forgive your trespasses."

St. Matthew 17:20, "And Jesus said unto them, Because of your unbelief: for verily I say unto you, **If** ye have faith as a grain of mustard seed, ye shall say unto this mountain, Remove hence to yonder place; and it shall remove; and nothing shall be impossible unto you."

St. Matthew 18:19, "Again I say unto you, That **if** two of you shall agree on earth as touching any thing that they shall ask, it shall be done for them of my Father which is in heaven."

St. Matthew 21:21, "Jesus answered and said unto them, Verily I say unto you, **If** ye have faith, and doubt not, ye shall not only do this which is done to the fig tree, but also **if** ye shall say unto this mountain, Be thou removed, and be thou cast into the sea; it shall be done."

St. Mark 9:23, "Jesus said unto him, **If** thou canst believe, all things are possible to him that believeth."

St. Mark 11:25, "And when ye stand praying, forgive, **if** ye have ought against any: that your Father also which is in heaven may forgive you your trespasses."

St. Mark 11:26, "But **if** ye do not forgive, neither will your Father which is in heaven forgive your trespasses."

St. Luke 16:11, "**If** therefore ye have not been faithful in the unrighteous mammon, who will commit to your trust the true riches?"

St. Luke 16:12, "And **if** ye have not been faithful in that which is another man's, who shall give you that which is your own?"

St. Luke 17:6, "And the Lord said, **If** ye had faith as a grain of mustard seed, ye might say unto this sycamine tree, Be thou plucked up by the root, and be thou planted in the sea; and it should obey you."

St. John 7:37, "In the last day, that great day of the feast, Jesus stood and cried, saying, **If** any man thirst, let him come unto me, and drink."

St. John 8:31, "Then said Jesus to those Jews which believed on him, **If** ye continue in my word, then are ye my disciples indeed;"

St. John 8:51, "Verily, verily, I say unto you, **If** a man keep my saying, he shall never see death."

St. John 12:26, "**If** any man serve me, let him follow me; and where I am, there shall also my servant be: **if** any man serve me, him will my Father honour."

St. John 12:32, "And I, **if** I be lifted up from the earth, will draw all men unto me."

St. John 14:14, "**If** ye shall ask any thing in my name, I will do it."

St. John 14:15, " **If** ye love me, keep my commandments."

St. John 14:23, "Jesus answered and said unto him, **If** a man love me, he will keep my words: and my Father will love him, and we will come unto him, and make our abode with him."

St. John 14:28, "Ye have heard how I said unto you, I go away, and come again unto you. **If** ye loved me, ye would rejoice, because I said, I go unto the Father: for my Father is greater than I."

St. John 15:6, "**If** a man abide not in me, he is cast forth as a branch, and is withered; and men gather them, and cast them into the fire, and they are burned."

St. John 15:7, "**If** ye abide in me, and my words abide in you, ye shall ask what ye will, and it shall be done unto you."

St. John 15:10, "**If** ye keep my commandments, ye shall abide in my love; even as I have kept my Father's commandments, and abide in his love."

St. John 15:14, "Ye are my friends, **if** ye do whatsoever I command you."

Romans 6:8, "Now **if** we be dead with Christ, we believe that we shall also live with him:"

Romans 8:9, "But ye are not in the flesh, but in the Spirit, **if** so be that the Spirit of God dwell in you. Now **if** any man have not the Spirit of Christ, he is none of his."

Romans 8:10, "And **if** Christ be in you, the body is dead because of sin; but the Spirit is life because of righteousness."

Romans 8:11, "But **if** the Spirit of him that raised up Jesus from the dead dwell in you, he that raised up Christ from the dead shall also quicken your mortal bodies by his Spirit that dwelleth in you." Romans 8:13, "For **if** ye live after the flesh, ye shall die: but **if** ye through the Spirit do mortify the deeds of the body, ye shall live."

Romans 8:17, "And **if** children, then heirs; heirs of God, and joint-heirs with Christ; **if** so be that we suffer with him, that we may be also glorified together."

Romans 8:31, "What shall we then say to these things? **If** God be for us, who can be against us?"

Romans 10:9, "That **if** thou shalt confess with thy mouth the Lord Jesus, and shalt believe in thine heart that God hath raised him from the dead, thou shalt be saved."

2 Corinthians 5:17, "Therefore **if** any man be in Christ, he is a new creature: old things are passed away; behold, all things are become new."

Galatians 6:1, "Brethren, **if** a man be overtaken in a fault, ye which are spiritual, restore such an one in the spirit of meekness; considering thyself, lest thou also be tempted."

Galatians 6:9, "And let us not be weary in well doing: for in due season we shall reap, **if** we faint not."

1 Thessalonians 3:8, "For now we live, **if** ye stand fast in the Lord."

2 Timothy 2:11, "It is a faithful saying: For **if** we be dead with him, we shall also live with him:"

2 Timothy 2:12, "**If** we suffer, we shall also reign with him: **if** we deny him, he also will deny us:"

2 Timothy 2:13, "**If** we believe not, yet he abideth faithful: he cannot deny himself."

Hebrews 3:14, "For we are made partakers of Christ, **if** we hold the beginning of our confidence stedfast unto the end;"

Hebrews 3:15, "While it is said, To day **if** ye will hear his voice, harden not your hearts, as in the provocation."

James 1:5, "**If** any of you lack wisdom, let him ask of God, that giveth to all men liberally, and upbraideth not; and it shall be given him."

James 1:23, "For **if** any be a hearer of the word, and not a doer, he is like unto a man beholding his natural face in a glass:"

James 1:26, "**If** any man among you seem to be religious, and bridleth not his tongue, but deceiveth his own heart, this man's religion is vain."

James 2:8, "**If** ye fulfil the royal law according to the scripture, Thou shalt love thy neighbour as thyself, ye do well:"

James 2:9, "But **if** ye have respect to persons, ye commit sin, and are convinced of the law as transgressors."
James 2:17, "Even so faith, **if** it hath not works, is dead, being alone."

James 4:15, "For that ye ought to say, **If** the Lord will, we shall live, and do this, or that."

1 Peter 4:11, "**If** any man speak, let him speak as the oracles of God; **if** any man minister, let him do it as of the ability which God giveth: that God in all things may be glorified through Jesus Christ, to whom be praise and dominion for ever and ever. Amen."

1 Peter 4:14, "**If** ye be reproached for the name of Christ, happy are ye; for the spirit of glory and of God resteth upon you: on their part he is evil spoken of, but on your part he is glorified."

1 Peter 4:16, "Yet **if** any man suffer as a Christian, let him not be ashamed; but let him glorify God on this behalf."

1 Peter 4:17, "For the time is come that judgment must begin at the house of God: and **if** it first begin at us, what shall the end be of them that obey not the gospel of God?"

1 Peter 4:18, "And **if** the righteous scarcely be saved, where shall the ungodly and the sinner appear?"

2 Peter 1:8, "For **if** these things be in you, and abound, they make you that ye shall neither be barren nor unfruitful in the knowledge of our Lord Jesus Christ."

2 Peter 1:10, "Wherefore the rather, brethren, give diligence to make your calling and election sure: for **if** ye do these things, ye shall never fall:"

1 John 1:6, "**If** we say that we have fellowship with him, and walk in darkness, we lie, and do not the truth:"

1 John 1:7, "But **if** we walk in the light, as he is in the light, we

have fellowship one with another, and the blood of Jesus Christ his Son cleanseth us from all sin."

1 John 1:8, "**If** we say that we have no sin, we deceive ourselves, and the truth is not in us."

1 John 1:9, "**If** we confess our sins, he is faithful and just to forgive us our sins, and to cleanse us from all unrighteousness."

1 John 1:10, "**If** we say that we have not sinned, we make him a liar, and his word is not in us."

1 John 2:1, "My little children, these things write I unto you, that ye sin not. And **if** any man sin, we have an advocate with the Father, Jesus Christ the righteous:"

1 John 2:3, "And hereby we do know that we know him, **if** we keep his commandments."

1 John 2:15, "Love not the world, neither the things that are in the world. **If** any man love the world, the love of the Father is not in him."

1 John 2:19, "They went out from us, but they were not of us; for **if** they had been of us, they would no doubt have continued with us: but they went out, that they might be made manifest that they were not all of us."

1 John 2:24, "Let that therefore abide in you, which ye have heard from the beginning. **If** that which ye have heard from the beginning shall remain in you, ye also shall continue in the Son,

and in the Father."

1 John 2:29, "**If** ye know that he is righteous, ye know that every one that doeth righteousness is born of him."

1 John 3:20, "For **if** our heart condemn us, God is greater than our heart, and knoweth all things."

1 John 3:21, "Beloved, **if** our heart condemns us not, then has we confidence toward God."

1 John 4:11, "Beloved, **if** God so loved us, we ought also to love one another."

1 John 4:12, "No man hath seen God at any time. **If** we love one another, God dwelleth in us, and his love is perfected in us."

1 John 5:14, "And this is the confidence that we have in him, that, **if** we ask any thing according to his will, he heareth us:"

1 John 5:15 KJV, "And **if** we know that he hear us, whatsoever we ask, we know that we have the petitions that we desired of him."

2 John 1:10, "**If** there come any unto you, and bring not this doctrine, receive him not into your house, neither bid him God speed:"

Revelations 3:20, "Behold, I stand at the door, and knock: **if** any man hear my voice, and open the door, I will come in to him, and will sup with him, and he with me."

Revelations 13:9, "**If** any man have an ear, let him hear."

Revelations 22:18, "For I testify unto every man that heareth the words of the prophecy of this book, **If** any man shall add unto these things, God shall add unto him the plagues that are written in this book:"

Revelations 22:19, "And **if** any man shall take away from the words of the book of this prophecy, God shall take away his part out of the book of life, and out of the holy city, and from the things which are written in this book."

Chapter Five

The Promises are unlocked by Faith!

ALL OF THE PROMISES OF GOD ARE RECEIVED BY FAITH

Can you believe God for the promises?

I believe in the sun – even when I cannot see it.
I believe in love, even when I cannot feel it.
I believe in God, even when He is silent.

It is easy for us to believe in those things that we can see, feel or hear, but we need to believe totally in God, even when we see no evidence. That is FAITH!

Hebrews 11:1, "Now **faith** is the substance of things hoped for, the evidence of things not seen."

Hebrews 11:3, "Through **faith** we understand that the worlds were framed by the word of God, so that things which are seen were not made of things which do appear."

Hebrews 11:4, "By **faith** Abel offered unto God a more excellent sacrifice than Cain, by which he obtained witness that he was righteous, God testifying of his gifts: and by it he being dead yet speaketh."

Hebrews 11:5, "By **faith** Enoch was translated that he should not see death; and was not found, because God had translated him: for before his translation he had this testimony, that he pleased God."

Hebrews 11:6, "But without **faith** it is impossible to please him: for he that cometh to God must believe that he is, and that he is a rewarder of them that diligently seek him."

Hebrews 11:7, "By **faith** Noah, being warned of God of things not seen as yet, moved with fear, prepared an ark to the saving of his house; by the which he condemned the world, and became heir of the righteousness which is by faith."

Hebrews 11:8, "By **faith** Abraham, when he was called to go out into a place which he should after receive for an inheritance, obeyed; and he went out, not knowing whither he went."

Hebrews 11:9, "By **faith** he sojourned in the land of promise, as in a strange country, dwelling in tabernacles with Isaac and Jacob, the heirs with him of the same promise:"

Hebrews 11:11, "Through **faith** also Sara herself received strength to conceive seed, and was delivered of a child when she was past age, because she judged him faithful who had promised."

Hebrews 11:13, "These all died in **faith**, not having received the promises, but having seen them afar off, and were persuaded of them, and embraced them, and confessed that they were strangers and pilgrims on the earth."

Hebrews 11:17, "By **faith** Abraham, when he was tried, offered up Isaac: and he that had received the promises offered up his only begotten son."

Hebrews 11:20, "By **faith** Isaac blessed Jacob and Esau concerning things to come."

Hebrews 11:21, "By **faith** Jacob, when he was a dying, blessed both the sons of Joseph; and worshipped, leaning upon the top of his staff."

Hebrews 11:22, "By **faith** Joseph, when he died, made mention of the departing of the children of Israel; and gave commandment concerning his bones."

Hebrews 11:23, "By **faith** Moses, when he was born, was hid three months of his parents, because they saw he was a proper child; and they were not afraid of the king's commandment."

Hebrews 11:24, "By **faith** Moses, when he was come to years, refused to be called the son of Pharaoh's daughter;"

Hebrews 11:27, "By **faith** he forsook Egypt, not fearing the wrath

of the king: for he endured, as seeing him who is invisible."
Hebrews 11:28, "Through **faith** he kept the Passover, and the
sprinkling of blood, lest he that destroyed the firstborn should
touch them."

Hebrews 11:29, "By **faith** they passed through the Red sea as by
dry land: which the Egyptians assaying to do were drowned."

Hebrews 11:30, "By **faith** the walls of Jericho fell down, after they
were compassed about seven days."

Hebrews 11:31, "By **faith** the harlot Rahab perished not with them
that believed not, when she had received the spies with peace."

Hebrews 11:33, "Who through **faith** subdued kingdoms, wrought
righteousness, obtained promises, stopped the mouths of lions,"

Hebrews 11:39, "And these all, having obtained a good report
through **faith**, received not the promise:"

Hebrews 12:2, "Looking unto Jesus the author and finisher of our
faith; who for the joy that was set before him endured the cross,
despising the shame, and is set down at the right hand of the throne
of God."

HOW TO LIVE WITH FAITH

*"What is faith? It is the confident assurance that what we hope for
is going to happen. It is the evidence of things we cannot yet see.
God gave his approval to people in days of old because of their
faith."* (Hebrews 11:1-2)

What does faith look like? Hebrews 11 provides living, breathing examples of faith. Abraham teaches us three actions of faith lived out.

1) FAITH LEAVES WHAT SEEMS FAMILIAR

"It was by faith that Abraham obeyed when God called him to leave home and go to another land that God would give him as his inheritance. He went without knowing where he was going." (Hebrews 11:8)

2) FAITH BELIEVES WHAT SEEMS IMPOSSIBLE

"It was by faith that Sarah together with Abraham was able to have a child, even though they were too old and Sarah was barren. Abraham believed that God would keep his promise." (Hebrews 11:11)

3) FAITH SURRENDERS WHAT SEEMS IRREPLACEABLE

"It was by faith that Abraham offered Isaac as a sacrifice when God was testing him. Abraham, who had received God's promises, was ready to sacrifice his only son, Isaac, though God had promised him, 'Isaac is the son through whom your descendants will be counted.' Abraham assumed that if Isaac died, God was able to bring him back to life again. And in a sense, Abraham did receive his son back from the dead." (Hebrews 11:17-19)

BUILDING A LIFE OF FAITH

"We can build a great life by walking and living by faith. All of us want to build great lives, and the Bible tells us how we can do that.

Do we get God's approval by becoming religious or going to church? No. Do we get God's approval by keeping the Ten Commandments? No. Do we get God's approval by being more good than bad? No. Do we get God's approval by promising to be perfect? No. The Bible says that there is only one way to get God's approval. There's only one way to get God's smile on your life. In the book of Hebrews, chapter 11, it says, "It is impossible to please God without faith" (Hebrews 11:6).

The only way you can get God's approval is through faith. You may be a great person, but without faith, it's impossible to please God. You may do all sorts of great things in your life, but without faith it's impossible to please God. God isn't interested in rules and rituals. He's only interested in one thing: that you develop a relationship of faith with Him. If you want to build a great life, it's essential that you know how to build a life of faith. Somebody has called faith the greatest power in the world.

What is faith? A lot of people have the wrong idea about what faith is. I've heard people say that faith is an irrational commitment to beliefs despite evidence to the contrary. I've heard others say that faith is like a blind leap into darkness. That's not faith; that's stupidity. Faith is actually the opposite. One could describe faith as a leap out of darkness back into the light. Faith is not irrational. It's based upon coherent and consistent reasoning. Faith isn't simplistic, but it is simple. Faith provides future hope for your soul.

What is faith? Probably the best definition of faith is found in Hebrews 11. As you have seen in a previous chapter, it's a book of the Bible that contains a list of people in the Bible who lived lives of faith. You could call it God's Hall of Faith. Hebrews 11:1 gives us a definition of faith. Hebrews 11:1 says, "What is faith? It is the confident assurance that what we hope for is going to happen. It is the evidence of things we cannot yet see." Here's a definition of faith. Faith is the <u>confident assurance</u> that God is in control of the future and that He will keep <u>His promises</u> to me because He has a purpose for me. Faith is building your life on the fact that God is in control, and that God will fulfill His promises even when you don't see those promises materializing.

Faith isn't making a good guess based on the best human estimate of what will happen. Faith isn't taking a leap of faith. Faith is believing the promises of God, even when there is nothing to show for it. God wants us to develop a life of faith.

There is one man in the Bible who stands out as a paragon of faith. His name is Abraham. Now, the great thing about Abraham is that he has been viewed throughout the centuries as a model of faith - not just by Christians but by two other religions. Muslims, Jews, and Christians all look to Abraham as a model of faith. In fact, Genesis 15:6 tell us, "And Abram believed the LORD, and the LORD declared him righteous because of his faith." Now, I like to look at Abraham's life because Abraham was as human as you and I are. Under pressure he told lies. Twice he gave away his wife to save his own life. But James 2:23 tells us that Abraham was called a friend of God. Despite all of his failures and all of his faults,

Abraham was called a friend of God. Why? Because of his faith. You don't have to be perfect to build a great life. But you do have to build a life of faith.

In Hebrews 11, no one person gets more attention than Abraham. In fact, Hebrews 11 mentions three episodes in Abraham's life that point to him as a man of faith. Let's look at these three episodes in Abraham's life and draw out three secrets on building a life of faith. The first secret is:

1. FAITH IS <u>OBEYING</u> EVEN WHEN YOU DON'T UNDERSTAND IT

You've got to obey even before you understand it. That's the first secret of developing a life of faith. Now, there are two types of people in this world. The first type is the spontaneous type. It never occurs to you to plan for the future, because the future isn't here yet. You're not worried about five minutes from now because you're simply in the moment. What I'm going to say now may not really apply to you.

But there's another group of people who like to have a little bit of security. That's me. I kind of like to know what I've got planned for the next week. Also, I like to know that when I leave where I am I've got a place to go home. Most of us, even if we're spontaneous, want to have a basic outline of the information involved before we make a big decision. We need to know how it's going to affect our lives.

I want you to meet Abraham. Hebrews 11:8-10:

"By faith Abraham, when called to go to a place he would later receive as his inheritance, he obeyed and went, even though he did not know where he was going. By faith he made his home in the Promised Land like a stranger in a foreign country; he lived in tents, as did Isaac and Jacob, who were heirs with him of the same promise. For he was looking forward to the city with foundations, whose architect and builder is God."

When we encounter Abraham in Hebrews 11:8, he's living in the area we would call Iraq today. He's 75 years old, and he's just getting ready for his old age pension. And then God comes along and tells him to move. God told him in Genesis 12:1, "Leave your country, your relatives, and your father's house, and go to the land that I will show you." Abraham says, "God, where am I going?" God says, "You've never heard of this place." Abraham says, "How long will it take to get there?" God says, "Don't worry about that." Abraham says, "How will I know when I'm there?" God says, "I'll tell you." God was asking Abraham to make a major move with very little information to go on.

Would you do it? Because Abraham obeyed even when he didn't understand it, he became the father of a nation called Israel. Many people were blessed because he obeyed even when it didn't make sense.

The problem with us isn't that we don't know what God's will is for us. The problem for us is that we lack the courage to go. We want all the information first. The first time God split a sea for His people, He caused the Red Sea to part before the people entered it. The second time that God split water for His people, He told them to enter the river and then He would split it. Sometimes God asks us to make the move before we have all the information.

Even when Abraham reached the land God promised him, he wasn't home free. Acts 7:5 tells us that when Abraham got to the land, "God gave him no inheritance here, not even one square foot of land." Abraham had to wait. Not only did he have to wait, but his children and grandchildren had to wait. Abraham risked all that he had for a promise. He risked all that he had and left it for the unknown, even though he didn't understand. Why? Because he had the confident assurance that God is in control of the future and that He will keep His promises.

Faith always involves risk. Some people want a guarantee of success before they obey God. They read something in the Bible and God tells them to do something and they say, "OK, God, once you guarantee it's going to work, then I'll do it." God says, "That doesn't require any faith. I want you to believe when you don't see it and I want you to obey when you don't understand it."

The New Testament contains 1,050 commands for us to obey. That's a lot of commands! I need to be really honest and tell you that sometimes I don't like all those commands. Do you? Some of them seem unreasonable. Some of them seem unusual. Some of them seem just plain inconvenient. It's tempting not to obey because I don't understand what's in it for me, or how God is going to provide if I keep that command.

Do you remember when your parents would ask you to do something that made no sense to you as a kid? You would say, "What do my parents know?" You thought that they were old fogies who didn't have a clue about life. Looking back, you can see the wisdom in what they told you. You were called to obey your parents even when you didn't understand. Now, as you look back, you can understand that your parents had a purpose in their requests. They did it out of love and concern for you.

God is far wiser and far more concerned about you than your parents. When you ignore His commands, you're a fool. It's foolish. He is the Creator. The Bible is the owner's manual for life. If you ignore it, who are you going to hurt? Not God. You're just going to hurt yourself.

You're going to build a life of faith and that's the foundation of building a great life. Here's the point: The foundation for building a life of great faith is learning to do whatever God tells you to do even when it seems absurd. When you subject yourself to obedience, God will truly bless your life.

On the other hand, if you ignore what God says to do – if you say, "I don't believe that stuff. I'm going to do what I think is best. I'm my own god," then you will miss out on all the great things and blessings that God has planned for your life and put you on this earth to enjoy. You'll miss them all.

In 1996 and 1997, I was faced with a decision that would alter my life. I had to choose between moving and leaving the ministry God told me to start and staying put and exiting the United States Air Force; losing almost 16 years of earned severance. Needless to say, I chose the latter. I was willing to get out of the military without any retirement or severance pay because I knew what God told me. To me, it was like a test. God was so gracious to cancel both assignments to New York and California and I retired from the United States Air Force after serving for 20 years and 4 days. God saw my faith, my trust, and my action to serve Him. I was willing to do something absurd. I was willing to obey even though I did not fully understand what God was doing.

I'm so glad now that I obeyed God at that point. If I had turned my back on what I knew God wanted me to do, I would have missed out on so many blessings. I wouldn't have had the opportunity to pastor one of the greatest churches on this side of heaven—Christian Fellowship Church. I wouldn't have had the pleasure of living in Warner Robins, Georgia. I wouldn't have had the joy of writing this book. I wouldn't have met so many wonderful friends. But it was simply an act of obedience. When you obey, even when you don't understand, God always honors that obedience.

What has God called you to do that you don't understand, and yet doing? Maybe you need to think about it today and say, "God, I'm through with waiting. Faith always involves risks. Today, I'm finally taking that step of obeying you even though I don't understand. Today I'm going to follow Abraham and make a move of obedience even when I don't understand." If you take this step, you won't miss the blessings that God has planned for your life.

There's a second secret that we need to understand if we're going to build a life of faith:

2. FAITH IS <u>BELIEVING</u> EVEN WHEN YOU CAN'T SEE IT

Have you ever thought about at least one thing that you thought was impossible for you to do? It could be anything – running a marathon or becoming a CEO or flying like a bird, but is there one thing that you really believe is impossible for you to do?

If you had stopped Abraham and Sarah thousands of years ago and asked them that question, you would have received one answer. They would have told you that it was impossible for them to have children. Now, it wasn't for lack of trying. They had tried and tried to have kids, and in fact they had given up so much hope that Sarah, Abraham's wife, gave him her servant to bear him a child when he was 86 years old. I think that Abraham and Sarah would have said, "There is no way on earth that we are ever going to have a child!"

The main problem with not having a son is that God had made a special promise – a covenant – with Abraham that involved Abraham having a son. This is a serious promise which assured that Abraham would become the father of many nations. His descendents would be countless and his descendents would have a "Promised Land." He was given all these wonderful incredible promises and this honor and blessing would come through his son. This is interesting because Abraham did not have a son. There's a time in the Bible when Abraham does one of those time-outs: "God, I appreciate all this but I don't have a son!" Abraham couldn't see a way that this could ever come true.

We need to realize that Abraham and Sarah both struggled with this dilemma. Have you ever felt that God has put your life on hold? That's how Abraham and Sarah felt. In fact, it got to the point where they didn't think that God had them on hold. They thought that God had hung up. It got to the point that when God told them they would have a child, Sarah laughed. I would have too. They were at the age of buying Depends, not Pampers. It was ludicrous to think that Abraham and Sarah would have a baby. But faith is believing even when you can't see it.

Abraham and Sarah weren't perfect in this struggle, but at age 100 Abraham gave birth to a son that God had promised him many years before. In spite of everyone's laughter, God's promise was born. Isaac was the dream child.

Hebrews 11:11-12:

"It was by faith that Sarah together with Abraham was able to have a child, even though they were too old and Sarah was barren. Abraham believed that God would keep his promise. And so a whole nation came from this one man, Abraham, who was too old to have any children—a nation with so many people that, like the stars of the sky and the sand on the seashore, there is no way to count them."

The key words in these verses are, "Abraham believed that God would keep His promise." Once again, faith is the confident assurance that God is in control of the future and that He will keep His promises to you because He has a purpose for you. God has a purpose for your life. God is absolutely committed to keeping His promises to you, even when you can't see them. You may be in a rush, but God isn't.

There are two principles that you need to understand to help you believe when it seems like God has put you on permanent hold. The first principle is this: **WAITING TIME IS NEVER WASTED TIME.** When God tells me what He wants to do, I can't wait to do it. On the other hand, God is seldom in a rush. Abraham had to wait until he was 100 years old. You may be waiting for God to do something. You may have given up. But God hasn't given up. God will keep His promises to you. Your waiting time is never wasted time.

What is God doing while we wait? A lot of things! God is maturing us in preparation for receiving the promise. God is testing us to see how committed we are to Him. God is working behind the scenes preparing the way. God is using circumstances to position and prepare you to accomplish His vision for your life. You may have to wait, but God's timing always has a purpose. God will fulfill His promises to you.

The other principle you need to understand, that will help you believe when you can't see God's promises being fulfilled, is this: **GOD IS NOT JUST THE GOD OF THE WHAT. GOD IS THE GOD OF THE HOW.** What do I mean by that? God specializes in the impossible. Someone once said, "What God originates, He orchestrates." I've found in my life that God always gives the what before He gives the how. He says, "Abraham, you're going to have a baby." Abraham's question was, "How?" God says, "Don't worry about the how, Abraham. I'll take care of the how. All you have to do is believe."

The problem with Abraham is that he couldn't see how it would take place, so he began working on his own plans just to help God out. I think Abraham figured, "God has given me the what. Now it's up to me to figure out how to do it." Every time Abraham took on the how part of the job, Abraham messed up. There's a reason: when God gives the what, he always gives the how. God specializes in doing the impossible. He wants to do something in your life that can only be explained by divine intervention.

God has a purpose in every experience that you've ever had. You may feel that right now, your life is on hold. You may be waiting for God to fulfill a promise that He gave you many years ago. You may be tempted not to believe, because you're tired of waiting. You need to know that God is in control of the future and that He will keep His promises to you because He has a purpose for you. God has a purpose in your waiting. He will take care of how it's going to happen – you don't have to. All you're called to do is to believe, even when you can't see it.

What is faith? It's obeying when I don't understand it. It believes when I don't see it. There's one more secret to developing a life of faith:

3. FAITH IS <u>GIVING</u> EVEN WHEN I CAN'T AFFORD IT

Giving and faith go together. And giving doesn't just involve money – it involves everything. Faith is all about giving God whatever we value most – whatever we possess and don't want to give up. Faith is about giving God our most valued possession – whether that's your money, your family, your reputation, or whatever. And the irony is that it's never really ours until we've given it to God.

One of the secrets of building a life of faith is found in Hebrews 11:17-19:

"It was by faith that Abraham was willing to offer Isaac as a sacrifice when God was testing him. Abraham, who had received God's promises, was ready to sacrifice his only son, Isaac, though God had promised him, "Isaac is the son through whom your descendants will be counted." Abraham assumed that if Isaac died, God was able to bring him back to life again. And in a sense, Abraham did receive his son back from the dead."

You may remember this story from when you were a child. This is probably one of the most confusing and troubling passages in the entire Bible. It doesn't make much sense until you begin to understand that God wasn't interested in a human sacrifice. God was interested in Abraham's heart. God gave Abraham this as a test. God wanted to test what was in Abraham's heart. He wanted to see if Abraham was willing to give when he couldn't afford to give. God was asking Abraham for the one thing that he couldn't afford to give, and Abraham had the faith to give it.

God isn't a mean or capricious God. God never asks us to sacrifice something for him without reason. But I will tell you this: if you want to build a life of faith, at some point you and God will do business on this issue of sacrifice. God isn't interested in being second in your life. He's only interested in first, and He won't settle for anything less. And God is asking you to make a sacrifice. The only question is, how are you going to respond?

Some of us say, "God, you provide, and then I'll sacrifice." That would be like Abraham saying that he would give up his son only when he knew he wouldn't have to. But that's not faith. It's like, "God, you bring in this big windfall and only when it arrives will I give some of it back to you." God says that may be gratitude but that certainly isn't faith.

Others of us say, "God, only take what's not important to me." But that's not faith either. I see this with my kids all the time. They have no problem sacrificing the things they didn't want in the first place. We say to God all the time, "God, take this and that. But leave my career alone. Don't ask me to sacrifice my money. Don't ask me to give up what matters most to me." And God says in return, "You don't understand. I'm not interested in those things. What I'm really interested in is your heart. And until you give me what matters most – whatever that is – you'll never really be sure that you've given me all."

The ironic part is that when we give God what matters most, God gives it right back. And when He doesn't give it back, it's only so that He can give us something much better. The minute Abraham gave Isaac to God, God said, "I didn't want him in the first place. You can have him back." Jesus said in Matthew 16:25, "If you try to keep your life for yourself, you will lose it. But if you give up your life for Me, you will find true life."

Corrie Ten Boom once commented that she learned to hold everything loosely in her hand, because she knew she would grasp them tightly and the Lord would have to pry her fingers away, and it would hurt. When we live with open hands, God doesn't have to pry our grip. God wants us to hold everything – whatever matters most – loosely, and to be prepared to give Him the very thing we think we can't afford to sacrifice. Why? Because faith is the confident assurance that God is in control of the future and that He will keep His promises to you because He has a purpose for you.

If you're afraid to trust God with your possessions, your dreams, or a person, then you need to pay attention to Abraham's example. Because Abraham was willing to give up everything for God, he received back far more than he could have imagined. You will never give up anything for God that God will not repay many times over. Jesus once said to his disciples:

I assure you that everyone who has given up house or brothers or sisters or mother or father or children or property, for my sake and for the Good News, will receive now in return, a hundred times over…And in the world to come they will have eternal life. (Mark 10:29-30)

Do you want to live a life of faith? Then you need to begin living today with the confident assurance that God is in control of the future and that He will keep His promises to us because He has a purpose for you. And that's going to involve obeying Him when you don't understand it, believing when you can't see it, and giving when you can't afford it. And it all begins today.

Somebody once said, "He is no fool who gives what he cannot keep in order to gain what he cannot lose." What is it that God is calling you to sacrifice for Him? What step of faith – of obedience - is he asking you to take today?"

If you are ready to obey and make the sacrifice pray this prayer, "Dear God, help me to be like Abraham and obey You even when I don't understand it. Help me to believe when I can't see it – when

I think it's impossible and hopeless. Help me to give when I can't afford it. Teach me to trust in You." Amen."

THE ONE YOU SERVE MAY BE THE ONE WHO GIVES YOU THE WORD YOU NEED

The Bible says that the LORD appeared to Abraham near the oak trees in Mamre and it was very hot that day. All of a sudden Abraham noticed that three men where standing in his view. He got up and ran to meet them, and he welcomed them by doing the customary bow.

Genesis 18:1, "And the LORD appeared unto him in the plains of Mamre: and he sat in the tent door in the heat of the day;"

Genesis 18:2, "And he lift up his eyes and looked, and, lo, three men stood by him: and when he saw them, he ran to meet them from the tent door, and bowed himself toward the ground,"

Genesis 18:3, "And said, My Lord, if now I have found favour in thy sight, pass not away, I pray thee, from thy servant:"

Genesis 18:4, "Let a little water, I pray you, be fetched, and wash your feet, and rest yourselves under the tree:"

Genesis 18:5, "And I will fetch a morsel of bread, and comfort ye your hearts; after that ye shall pass on: for therefore are ye come to your servant. And they said, So do, as thou hast said."

Genesis 18:6, "And Abraham hastened into the tent unto Sarah, and said, Make ready quickly three measures of fine meal, knead it, and make cakes upon the hearth."

Genesis 18:7, "And Abraham ran unto the herd, and fetched a calf tender and good, and gave it unto a young man; and he hasted to dress it."

Genesis 18:8, "And he took butter, and milk, and the calf which he had dressed, and set it before them; and he stood by them under the tree, and they did eat."

Genesis 18:9, "And they said unto him, Where is Sarah thy wife? And he said, Behold, in the tent."

Genesis 18:10, "And he said, I will certainly return unto thee according to the time of life; and, lo, Sarah thy wife shall have a son. And Sarah heard it in the tent door, which was behind him."

Abraham was very courtesy and polite. He greeted the three men who were passing through and welcomed them by offering to wash their feet. He also offered to prepare some food to refresh them. He asked them to stay awhile before continuing their travel. And when the men agreed to stay awhile, he ran back to his tent and asked his wife to get the best grub she could find. Abraham then ran out and told his servant to find the best cow and butcher it. When the food was ready, Abraham served it to the three men. Now here's the blessing! After the men ate and enjoyed the food, they asked, where is Sarah, your wife?" You may ask, now, why would they want to know where his wife was? Here is why: One of them said, "About this time next year I will return, and your wife Sarah will have a son."

The same men whom Abraham served gave him a Rhema word! A word that had been already spoken by God before! Knowing about God's promise, Abraham continued to serve. We must continue to serve because the same one that we serve may have the word that we need to keep us going. Who is it that has a word for you? You may never know if you don't continue to serve. Many are praying, pleading, begging, crying, asking, worrying but not **SERVING**! Even though you may know what the promise is or the promises are, you must continue in your **SERVING**. The next person you serve may just have the word you need that will boost you to your blessed place. **SERVING** will lead you to your **PROMISE**!

CHAPTER SIX

THERE IS NOTHING TOO HARD FOR GOD

IS THERE ANYTHING TOO HARD FOR GOD?

Genesis 18:11, "Now Abraham and Sarah were old and well stricken in age; and it ceased to be with Sarah after the manner of women."

Genesis 18:12, "Therefore Sarah laughed within herself, saying, After I am waxed old shall I have pleasure, my lord being old also?"

Genesis 18:13, "And the LORD said unto Abraham, Wherefore did Sarah laugh, saying, Shall I of a surety bear a child, which am old?"

Genesis 18:14, "**Is any thing too hard for the LORD?** At the time appointed I will return unto thee, according to the time of life, and Sarah shall have a son."

Genesis 18:15, "Then Sarah denied, saying, I laughed not; for she was afraid. And he said, Nay; but thou didst laugh."

As the men spoke to Abraham, we find Sarah ease dropping. She was listening as the men spoke to her husband. She began to think—like some of us do, well Abraham is old and I am too. So, how in the world is God going to pull this off? Isn't that like us?

- Does God know how old we are?
- Does God know my situation?
- Does God know my circumstances?
- Does God know my lack of abilities?
- Does God know my education level?
- Does God know my financial status?
- Does God know who my parents are?
- Does God know it's too late?
- Does God know where we are at this time and place in life?

People all over the world can come up with all kinds of excuses, issues, and reasons why they cannot do what God says they can do.

I don't believe Sarah understood the promise God made. First of all, the question is who are you? What does your name mean? Abram means, "Exalted father." Abraham means "father of many." Sarah means "princess." Even though God had promise Abraham he would be the father of many, he was not yet father of any. Even though God made Sarah a princess, she didn't feel like a princess. This is most of our problems: We walk with feeling and not by faith. We walk by what we see and not by what has been said. If God has spoken it, He is able to perform it. Paul said in Romans 4:21, "And being fully persuaded that, what He had promised, He was able also to perform."

The Word of God asked, **"Is any thing too hard for 'Jehovah?'"** Jehovah is the Self-Existent God. He is the only Uncaused Cause. He is unchanging. He is omnipotent; He has all power! If He said He would do it, He will do it—no matter how hard it looks to the human eye. It may even be incomprehensive to the human mind, but if God said He would do it; it's done!

For some people, they can't see beyond what they can see. They might have physical sight but they don't have vision. That's why I believe that all of the promises of God are received by faith. For the Scriptures clearly declares in 2 Corinthians 5:7, "For we walk by faith, not by sight:"

Jeremiah 32:17, "Ah Lord GOD! behold, thou hast made the heaven and the earth by thy great power and stretched out arm, and there is nothing **too hard** for thee:"

Jeremiah 32:27, "Behold, I am the LORD, the God of all flesh: **is there any thing too hard** for me?"

I am convinced! There is nothing too hard for GOD!

Even though things look the way they are, they may not be as though they seem! Sarah looked at herself and then she looked at her husband and said, "How could a worn-out woman like me have a baby?" She thought. What she didn't know is that God was about to do something so miraculous that would make her laugh. Have you ever had God to do something so great in your life that made you laugh? Well, He can, and He will! Just as he made Sarah laugh, He can make you laugh. God asked Abraham why did his wife question the promise and why did she laugh about it. The Lord told him, "About a year from now, just as I told you, I will return, and Sarah will have a son." If you have read the story, you know that Sarah tried to deny that she had laughed because God saw it and heard it. She was afraid or shall I say had reverential fear because God knew what she had done. She did laugh just like many of us would have laughed because from where we sit it seems impossible. When it was all said and done, she named her son Isaac which means, "he laughs." After all the laughing is done, God will get the last laugh.

AS THE LORD WAS WITH JOSEPH SO WILL HE BE WITH YOU!

Genesis 39:2, "And **the LORD was with Joseph**, and he was a prosperous man; and he was in the house of his master the Egyptian."

Genesis 39:21, "But **the LORD was with Joseph**, and showed him mercy, and gave him favour in the sight of the keeper of the prison."

We picture Joseph as a servant to Potiphar in Ancient Egypt. Egypt was a place of great dissimilarity. "People were either rich beyond measure or poverty stricken. There wasn't much middle ground. Joseph found himself serving Potiphar, an extremely rich officer in Pharaoh's service. Rich families like Potiphar's had elaborate homes two or three stories tall with beautiful gardens and balconies. They enjoyed live entertainment at home as they chose delicious fruit from expensive bowls. They surrounded themselves with alabaster vases, paintings, beautiful rugs, and hand-carved chairs. Dinner was served on golden tableware, and the rooms were lighted with golden candlesticks. Servants, like Joseph, worked on the first floor, while the family occupied the upper stories."

Digressing, let's go back to the 37th Chapter of Genesis. We find Joseph having dreams which is how this incipient story begins. Joseph had a number of events that took place in his dreams that upset his family. The initial plan was to kill Joseph and cast him into a deep pit, but because of his older brother Ruben Joseph was spared. When they saw a company of Ishmaelites they sold Joseph and the traders took him to Egypt. To dupe their Father, Joseph's brothers killed a goat and dipped his coat in its blood. They lied and said they had found Joseph's coat in the field and believed that he was killed by a wild animal. Meanwhile, back in Egypt, we find the arrival of Joseph; he was purchased by Potiphar, a member of the personal staff of Pharaoh, the king of Egypt. Potiphar was the captain of the palace guard.

In Genesis the 39th Chapter, the Bible says **that The LORD was with Joseph and blessed him greatly** as he served in the home of his Egyptian master. Potiphar noticed and realized that the LORD was with Joseph, giving him success in everything he did. Joseph had favor in every area of his life. The hand of God was on Joseph's life, Potiphar allowed Joseph to be in charge of his entire household and entrusted him with all his business dealings.

BLESSED BY ASSOCIATION!

Due to Joseph being in Potiphar's house, Potiphar was blessed tremendously. All his household affairs began to run smoothly, and his crops and livestock flourished. Consequently, Potiphar gave Joseph complete managerial responsibility over everything he owned. With Joseph there, he didn't have a concern in the world, except to decide what he wanted to eat!

Even though Joseph was cast into prison because of a fabricated story, the LORD was with him! God granted Joseph favor with the chief jailer. The chief jailer eventually put Joseph in charge of all the other prisoners and over everything that happened in the prison. The chief jailer had no more worries after that, because Joseph took care of everything. The LORD was with Joseph, making everything run smoothly and successfully. Interesting point to note, everyone that Joseph came in contact with whether they where godly or ungodly, saved or unsaved, righteous or unrighteous, holy or unholy, real or fake, young or old, rich or poor, blessed or unblessed benefited from his presence because God was with him. We can conclude that if God is there, there is a possibility that everything is going to be alright! Nine proofs God promises will not fail...

1. The Lord was with Joseph when his brother's got angry with him.
2. The Lord was with Joseph when his brother's were jealous of him.
3. The Lord was with Joseph when he was thrown into a pit.
4. The Lord was with Joseph when he was sold into slavery.

5. The Lord was with Joseph when he was pressured and solicited for sex.
6. The Lord was with Joseph when he was lied on by Potiphar's wife.
7. The Lord was with Joseph when he was put in prison unjustly.
8. The Lord was with Joseph when the cup-bearer forgot about him after he interpreted his dream.
9. The Lord was with Joseph when Pharaoh made Joseph ruler over Egypt.

As God was with Joseph, He will be with you also! Remember, when people or the events of life come against you, God is with you! When others lie on you—God is with you. When others are jealous of you—God is with you. When others have been drinking "hater-ade" and they hate on you—God is with you. When seemingly everything is coming against you remember—God is with you!

KNOWLEDGE WILL GIVE YOU INSIGHT TO THE PROMISES OF GOD

NUGGETS ON KNOWLEDGE:

Knowledge aids in destroying the fear of the unknown, misinformation, false teaching and bad tradition.

Knowledge is the gateway to deliverance.

Knowledge is the vehicle that leads us when we are in our deliberation process.

Knowledge without revelation is just information.

Knowledge frees us to move forward without hesitation during our decision making process.

Knowledge is facts needed in order to make sound judgment that will bring increase.

Knowledge opens us and challenges us to try things we have never entertained or tried before.

Knowledge opens new doors to us and gives us courage to explore what's behind them.

Knowledge helps us to create and build divine ideas given to us by the Lord.

Knowledge destroys myths, counterfeits, and falsehoods.

Knowledge cast down doubt and increases belief.

Knowledge keeps secrets and never forgets!

Knowledge comes from above and spreads to those who will embrace it.

Knowledge brings new cultivation.

Knowledge warns us of things that are about to happen which have already happened.

Knowledge is more than information, education, and communication; it is revelation.

Without **Knowledge** there will be much intimidation!

Knowledge is more than scholastic academics, being cleverly astute, philosophically eloquent and intellectually perceptive; it is knowing the Wisdom of God.

Knowledge flows through and from generations to generations.

Knowledge enriches!

Knowledge will broaden your borders.

Knowledge lives!

Knowledge comes from God.

Proverbs 2:1-6, "My son, if thou wilt receive my words, and hide my commandments with thee; So that thou incline thine ear unto wisdom, and apply thine heart to understanding; Yea, if thou criest after **knowledge**, and liftest up thy voice for understanding; If thou seekest her as silver, and searchest for her as for hidden treasures; Then shalt thou understand the fear of the LORD, and find the **knowledge** of God. For the LORD giveth wisdom: out of his mouth cometh **knowledge** and understanding."

The **Knowledge of God** leads to God's promises!

Chapter Seven

Great Promises from the Bible

Unfailing

1 Kings 8:56, "Blessed be the LORD that hath given rest unto his people Israel, according to all that he promised: **there hath not failed one word of all his good promise, which he promised** by the hand of Moses his servant."

Assured by Divine Ability

Romans 4:21, "And being fully persuaded that, what he had promised, **he was able also to perform**."

Grounded in Christ

2 Corinthians 1:20, "For all the **promises** of God in him are yea, and in him Amen, unto the glory of God by us."

Of Infinite Value

2 Peter 1:4, "Whereby are **given unto us exceeding great and precious promises:** that by these ye might be partakers of the divine nature, having escaped the corruption that is in the world through lust."

Culminate in Everlasting Life

1 John 2:25, "And this is the **promise** that he hath **promised** us, even eternal life."

Desires Given

Psalm 37:4, "Delight thyself also in the LORD; and he shall **give thee the desires of thine heart**."

Addition to Your Life

St. Matthew 6:33, "But seek ye first the kingdom of God, and his righteousness; and all these things shall be **added** unto you."

Prosperity and pleasures

Job 36:11, "If they obey and serve him, they shall spend their days in **prosperity**, and their years in **pleasures**."

Have the Best Part

Isaiah 1:19, "If ye be willing and obedient, ye shall eat the **good** of the land:

Ways Opened and a Great Pouring and Flowing

Malachi 3:10, "Bring ye all the tithes into the storehouse, that there may be meat in mine house, and prove me now herewith, saith the LORD of hosts, if I will not **open you the windows** of heaven, and **pour you out a blessing**, that there shall **not be room enough to receive it**."

Good Measure, Pressed Down, and Shaken Together

St. Luke 6:38, "Give, and it shall be given unto you; **good measure, pressed down, and shaken together**, and running over, shall men give into your bosom. For with the same measure that ye mete withal it shall be measured to you again."

Ask, Seek, and Knock—Given, Find, and Opened

St. Matthews 7:7, "**Ask**, and it shall be **given** you; **seek**, and ye shall **find**; **knock**, and it shall be **opened** unto you:"

St. Luke 11:9, "And I say unto you, **Ask**, and it shall be **given** you; **seek**, and ye shall **find**; **knock**, and it shall be **opened** unto you."

Strength Renewed

Isaiah 40:31, "But they that wait upon the LORD shall **renew their strength**; they shall mount up with wings as eagles; they shall run, and not be weary; and they shall walk, and not faint."

PROMISES TO THE AFFLICTED:

Brighter Days

Psalms 30:5, "For his anger endureth but a moment; in his favour is life: weeping may endure for a night, but **joy** cometh in the morning."

Deliverance

Psalms 34:19, "Many are the afflictions of the righteous: but the LORD **delivereth** him out of them all."

Psalms 34:20, "He **keepeth** all his bones: not one of them is broken."

Divine Care in Sickness

Psalms 41:3, "The LORD will **strengthen** him upon the bed of languishing: thou wilt **make all his bed** in his sickness."

Psalms 50:15, "And call upon me in the day of trouble: I will **deliver** thee, and thou shalt glorify me."

Psalms 94:12, "**Blessed** is the man whom thou chastenest, O LORD, and teachest him out of thy law;"

Psalms 138:7, "Though I walk in the midst of trouble, thou wilt **revive** me: thou shalt stretch forth thine hand against the wrath of mine enemies, and thy right hand shall **save** me."

Comfort of God's Presence

Isaiah 43:2, "When thou passest through the waters, **I will be with thee**; and through the rivers, they shall not overflow thee: when thou walkest through the fire, thou shalt not be burned; neither shall the flame kindle upon thee."

An Eternal Home

St. John 14:1, "Let not your heart be troubled: ye believe in God, believe also in me."

St. John 14:2, "In my Father's house are **many mansions**: if it were not so, I would have told you. I go to prepare a place for you."

All Things Work for the Believer's Good

Romans 8:28, "And we know that all **things work together for good** to them that love God, to them who are the called according to his purpose."

2 Corinthians 4:17, "For our light affliction, which is but for a moment, **worketh for us a far more** exceeding and eternal weight of glory;"

Sufficiency of Divine Grace

2 Corinthians 12:9, "And he said unto me, My **grace is sufficient** for thee: for my strength is made perfect in weakness. Most gladly

therefore will I rather glory in my infirmities, that the power of Christ may rest upon me."

Fellowship in Christ's Sufferings

1 Peter 4:12, "Beloved, think it not strange concerning the fiery trial which is to try you, as though some strange thing happened unto you:"

1 Peter 4:13, "But rejoice, inasmuch as ye are **partakers of Christ's sufferings**; that, when his glory shall be revealed, ye may be glad also with exceeding joy."

Membership in the Company of the Redeemed

Revelations 7:13, "And one of the elders answered, saying unto me, What are these which are arrayed in white robes? and whence came they?"

Revelations 7:14, "And I said unto him, Sir, thou knowest. And he said to me, **These are they** which came out of great tribulation, and have washed their robes, and made them white in the blood of the Lamb."

Final Deliverance from Sorrow and Pain

Revelations 21:4, "And God shall **wipe away all tears** from their eyes; and there shall be no more death, neither sorrow, nor crying, neither shall there be any more pain: for the former things are passed away."

PROMISES TO BELIEVERS:

Bodily Supplies

Psalms 37:3, "Trust in the LORD, and do good; so shalt thou dwell in the land, and verily thou shalt be **fed**."

Unlimited Blessings

St. Mark 9:23, "Jesus said unto him, If thou canst believe, **all things are possible** to him that believeth."

Answers to Prayer

St. Mark 11:24, "Therefore I say unto you, What things soever ye **desire**, when ye **pray**, **believe** that ye **receive** them, and ye **shall have them**."

Removal of Obstacles

St. Luke 17:6, "And the Lord said, If ye had faith as a grain of mustard seed, ye might say unto this sycamine tree, Be thou plucked up by the root, and be thou planted in the sea; and it should **obey you**."

Divine Sonship

St. John 1:12, "But as many as received him, to them gave he power to become the **sons of God**, even to them that believe on his name:"

Eternal Life

St. John 3:14, "And as Moses lifted up the serpent in the wilderness, even so must the Son of man be lifted up:"

St. John 3:15, "That whosoever believeth in him should not perish, but have **eternal life**.

St. John 5:24, "Verily, verily, I say unto you, He that heareth my word, and believeth on him that sent me, hath **everlasting life**, and shall not come into condemnation; but is passed from death unto life."

Spiritual Fullness

St. John 6:35, "And Jesus said unto them, I am the bread of life: he that cometh to me shall **never hunger**; and he that believeth on me shall **never thirst**."

St. John 11:26, "And whosoever liveth and believeth in me shall **never die**. Believest thou this?"

Spiritual Light

St. John 12:46, "I am come a **light** into the world, that whosoever believeth on me should not abide in darkness.

Power for Service

St. John 14:12, "Verily, verily, I say unto you, He that believeth on me, the works that I do shall he do also; and **greater works** than these shall he do; because I go unto my Father."

Salvation

Romans 1:16, "For I am not ashamed of the Gospel of Christ: for it is the power of God unto **salvation** to every one that believeth; to the Jew first, and also to the Greek."

1 Peter 2:6, "Wherefore also it is contained in the scripture, Behold, I lay in Sion a chief corner stone, elect, precious: and he that believeth on him **shall not be confounded**."

PROMISES TO THE HUMBLE:

Respect

Psalms 138:6, "Though the LORD be high, yet hath he **respect** unto the lowly: but the proud he knoweth afar off."

Watch Over You

Isaiah 66:2, "For all those things hath mine hand made, and all those things have been, saith the LORD: but **to this man will I look**, even to him that is poor and of a contrite spirit, and trembleth at my word."

The Least shall be Great

St. Luke 9:48, "And said unto them, Whosoever shall receive this child in my name receiveth me: and whosoever shall receive me receiveth him that sent me: for he that is least among you all, the same **shall be great**."

Exaltation

St. Luke 4:11, "For whosoever exalteth himself shall be abased; and he that humbleth himself shall be **exalted**."

Grace Given

James 4:6, "But he giveth more **grace**. Wherefore he saith, God resisteth the proud, but giveth grace unto the humble."

1 Peter 5:5, "Likewise, ye younger, submit yourselves unto the elder. Yea, all of you be subject one to another, and be clothed with humility: for God resisteth the proud, and giveth **grace** to the humble."

PROMISES TO THE LIBERAL:

Delivered Out of Trouble

Psalms 41:1, "To the chief Musician, A Psalm of David. Blessed is he that considereth the poor: the LORD will **deliver** him in time of trouble."

Filled with Plenty

Proverbs 3:9, "Honour the LORD with thy substance, and with the firstfruits of all thine increase:"

Proverbs 3:10, "So shall thy barns be **filled with plenty**, and thy presses shall burst out with new wine."

Giving brings Increase, Blessings coming back Multiplied

Proverbs 11:25, "The liberal soul shall be made **fat**: and he that watereth shall be **watered** also himself."

Sharing brings Blessings

Proverbs 22:9, "He that hath a bountiful eye shall be **blessed**; for he giveth of his bread to the poor.

No Lack

Proverbs 28:27, "He that giveth unto the poor shall **not lack**: but he that hideth his eyes shall have many a curse.

Blessings coming back multiplied

Ecclesiastes 11:1, "Cast thy bread upon the waters: for thou **shalt find** it after many days."

Light Shined Upon You

Isaiah 58:10, "And if thou draw out thy soul to the hungry, and satisfy the afflicted soul; then shall thy **light rise** in obscurity, and thy darkness be as the noon day:"

Overflow of Blessings

St. Luke 6:38, "Give, and it shall be given unto you; good measure, pressed down, and shaken together, and **running over**, shall men give into your bosom. For with the same measure that ye mete withal it shall be measured to you again."

Recompensed

St. Luke 14:14, "And thou shalt be blessed; for they cannot recompense thee: for thou shalt be **recompensed** at the resurrection of the just."

God's Love Continuously Flowing

2 Corinthians 9:7, "Every man according as he purposeth in his heart, so let him give; not grudgingly, or of necessity: for **God loveth** a cheerful giver."

PROMISES TO THE OBEDIENT:

Mercy Shown

Exodus 20:6, "And **showing mercy** unto thousands of them that love me, and keep my commandments."

God will Side with You

Exodus 23:22, "But if thou shalt indeed obey his voice, and do all that I speak; then **I will be an enemy unto thine enemies**, and an adversary unto thine adversaries."

Go Well with You and Your Children

Deuteronomy 4:40, "Thou shalt keep therefore his statutes, and his commandments, which I command thee this day, that **it may go well with thee, and with thy children after thee**, and that thou mayest prolong thy days upon the earth, which the LORD thy God giveth thee, for ever."

Blessed with A Blessing

Deuteronomy 11:27, "**A blessing**, if ye obey the commandments of the LORD your God, which I command you this day:"

Building with a Sure House

1 Kings 11:38, "And it shall be, if thou wilt hearken unto all that I command thee, and wilt walk in my ways, and do that is right in my sight, to keep my statutes and my commandments, as David my servant did; that I will be with thee, and **build thee a sure house,** as I built for David, and will give Israel unto thee."

Eat Good

Isaiah 1:19, "If ye be willing and obedient, ye shall **eat the good** of the land:"

~91~

Part of God's Family

St. Mark 3:35, "For whosoever shall do the will of God, **the same is my brother, and my sister, and mother.**"

Blessed for Keeping and Acting upon God's Word

St. Luke 11:28, "But he said, Yea rather, **blessed are they** that hear the word of God, and keep it."

Knowledge Known

St. John 7:17, "If any man will do his will, **he shall know** of the doctrine, whether it be of God, or whether I speak of myself."

Life with Christ

St. John 14:23, "Jesus answered and said unto him, If a man love me, he will keep my words: and my Father will love him, and we will come unto him, and **make our abode** with him."

PROMISES TO THE PENITENT:

God is Near

Psalms 34:18, "The LORD is **nigh** unto them that are of a broken heart; and saveth such as be of a contrite spirit."

Will Heal Backslidings

Jeremiah 3:22, "Return, ye backsliding children, and I will **heal your backslidings**. Behold, we come unto thee; for thou art the LORD our God."

Gives Grace, Mercy, and Kindness

Joel 2:13, "And rend your heart, and not your garments, and turn unto the LORD your God: for he is **gracious** and **merciful**, slow to anger, and of great **kindness**, and repenteth him of the evil."

Micah 7:18, "Who is a God like unto thee, that **pardoneth iniquity**, and **passeth by** the transgression of the remnant of his heritage? he retaineth not his anger for ever, because he delighteth in **mercy**."

Turn your Weeping into Laughter

St. Luke 6:21, "Blessed are ye that hunger now: for ye shall be filled. Blessed are ye that weep now: for ye shall **laugh**."

St. Luke 15:7, "I say unto you, that likewise **joy** shall be in heaven over one sinner that repenteth, more than over ninety and nine just persons, which need no repentance."

Gift of the Holy Ghost

Acts 2:38, "Then Peter said unto them, Repent, and be baptized every one of you in the name of Jesus Christ for the remission of sins, and ye shall receive the **gift of the Holy Ghost**."

Times of Refreshing

Acts 3:19, "Repent ye therefore, and be converted, that your sins may be blotted out, when the **times of refreshing** shall come from the presence of the Lord;"

PROMISES TO THE POOR:

Saveth

Job 5:15, "But he **saveth** the poor from the sword, from their mouth, and from the hand of the mighty."

Safety

Psalms 12:5, "For the oppression of the poor, for the sighing of the needy, now will I arise, saith the LORD; I will set him in **safety** from him that puffeth at him."

Refuge

Psalms 14:6, "Ye have shamed the counsel of the poor, because the LORD is his **refuge**."

Goodness

Psalms 68:10, "Thy congregation hath dwelt therein: thou, O God, hast prepared of thy **goodness** for the poor."

Heard

Psalms 69:33, "For the LORD **heareth** the poor, and despiseth not his prisoners."

Right Hand of Honor

Psalms 109:31, "For he shall stand at the **right hand** of the poor, to save him from those that condemn his soul."

Psalms 140:12, "I know that the LORD will maintain the cause of the afflicted, and the **right of** the poor."

Righteousness and Equity

Isaiah 11:4, "But with **righteousness** shall he judge the poor, and reprove with **equity** for the meek of the earth: and he shall smite the earth with the rod of his mouth, and with the breath of his lips shall he slay the wicked."

An Overshadowing Providence

Isaiah 25:4, "For thou hast been a **strength** to the poor, a **strength** to the needy in his distress, a **refuge** from the storm, a **shadow** from the heat, when the blast of the terrible ones is as a storm against the wall.

Answer to Prayer

Isaiah 41:17, "When the poor and needy seek water, and there is none, and their tongue faileth for thirst, I **the LORD will hear**

them, I the God of Israel will not forsake them."

Heavenly Inheritance

James 2:5, "Hearken, my beloved brethren, Hath not God chosen the poor of this world rich in faith, and **heirs of the kingdom** which he hath **promised** to them that love him?"

PROMISES TO SEEKERS:

Deuteronomy 4:29, "But if from thence thou shalt **seek** the LORD thy God, thou shalt find him, if thou **seek** him with all thy heart and with all thy soul."

2 Chronicles 7:14, "If my people, which are called by my name, shall **humble** themselves, and **pray**, and **seek** my face, and **turn** from their wicked ways; then will I **hear** from heaven, and will **forgive** their sin, and will **heal** their land."

Proverbs 8:17, "I love them that love me; and those that **seek** me early shall find me."

Jeremiah 29:13, "And ye shall **seek** me, and find me, when ye shall **search** for me with all your heart."

St. Luke 11:9, "And I say unto you, **Ask**, and it shall be **given** you; **seek**, and ye shall **find**; **knock**, and it shall be **opened** unto you."
St. Luke 18:7, "And shall not God **avenge** his own elect, which cry day and night unto him, though he bear long with them?"

St. John 14:14, "If ye shall **ask** any thing in my name, I will do it."

PROMISES TO THE TEMPTED:

Power to Tread on Evil Forces

St. Luke 10:19, "Behold, I give unto you **power** to tread on serpents and scorpions, and over all the **power** of the enemy: and nothing shall by any means hurt you."

Safety through Christ's Intercession

St. Luke 22:31, "And the **Lord said**, Simon, Simon, behold, Satan hath desired to have you, that he may sift you as wheat:"

St. Luke 22:32, "But **I have prayed for thee**, that thy faith fail not: and when thou art converted, strengthen thy brethren."

The Bruising of the Serpent's Head

Romans 16:20, "And the God of peace shall **bruise Satan under your feet** shortly. The grace of our Lord Jesus Christ be with you. Amen."

Provision of a Way of Escape

1 Corinthians 10:13, "There hath no temptation taken you but such as is common to man: but God is faithful, who will not suffer you to be tempted above that ye are able; but will with the temptation also **make a way to escape**, that ye may be able to bear it."

Succor in the Trying Hour

Hebrews 2:18, "For in that he himself hath suffered being tempted, he is able to **succour** them that are tempted."

Final Victory

James 4:7, "Submit yourselves therefore to God. Resist the devil, and **he will flee from you.**"

Enthronement with Christ

Revelations 3:21, "To him that overcometh will I grant to sit with me in my **throne**, even as I also overcame, and am set down with my Father in his **throne**."

PROMISES TO THE WORKERS:

Shine forth and Convert Many

Daniel 12:3, "And they that be wise shall **shine** as the brightness of the firmament; and they that **turn** many to righteousness as the stars for ever and ever."

Great Reward

St. Mark 9:41, "For whosoever shall give you a cup of water to drink in my name, because ye belong to Christ, verily I say unto you, he shall not lose his reward."

Glory, Honor, and Peace

Romans 2:10, "But glory, honour, and peace, to every man that **worketh** good, to the Jew first, and also to the Gentile:"

Receive a Reward

1 Corinthians 3:14, "If any man's **work** abide which he hath built thereupon, he shall **receive a reward**."

Labor will Payoff

1 Corinthians 15:58, "Therefore, my beloved brethren, be ye stedfast, unmoveable, always abounding in the **work** of the Lord, forasmuch as ye know that your **labour is not in vain in the Lord**."

Not Forgotten by the Lord

Hebrews 6:10, "For God is **not** unrighteous to **forget your work and labour of love**, which ye have showed toward his name, in that ye have ministered to the saints, and do minister."

Blessed in your deeds

James 1:25, "But whoso looketh into the perfect law of liberty, and continueth therein, he being not a forgetful hearer, but a doer of the work, this man shall be **blessed in his deed**."

ABUNDANCE PROMISED:

Abundant Joys

Psalms 36:8, "They shall be **abundantly satisfied** with the fatness of thy house; and thou shalt make them drink of the river of thy pleasures."

Abundant Life

St. John 10:10, "The thief cometh not, but for to steal, and to kill, and to destroy: I am come that they might have life, and that they might have it **more abundantly**."

Abundant Grace

2 Corinthians 9:8, "And God is **able** to make all grace **abound** toward you; that ye, always having **all sufficiency** in **all things**, may **abound** to every good work:"

Abundant Power

Ephesians 3:20, "Now unto him that is **able** to do **exceeding abundantly** above all that we ask or think, according to the **power** that worketh in us,"

Abundant Supplies

Philippians 4:19, "But my God shall **supply all** your need according to his riches in glory by Christ Jesus."

Abundant Entrance

2 Peter 1:11, "For so an **entrance** shall be ministered unto you **abundantly** into the everlasting kingdom of our Lord and Saviour Jesus Christ."

PLENTY PROMISED:

Full

Leviticus 26:5, "And your threshing shall reach unto the vintage, and the vintage shall reach unto the sowing time: and ye shall eat your bread to the **full**, and dwell in your land safely."

Every Work

Deuteronomy 30:9, "And the LORD thy God will make thee **plenteous** in **every work** of thine hand, in the fruit of thy body, and in the fruit of thy cattle, and in the fruit of thy land, for good: for the LORD will again rejoice over thee for good, as he rejoiced over thy fathers:"

No Failure

Joshua 21:45, "**Not one of all the Lord's good promises** to the house of Israel **failed**; **every one was fulfilled**." *(New International Version)*

Joshua 23:14, "Now I am about to go the way of all the earth. You know with all your heart and soul that **not one of all the good promises the LORD your God gave you has failed**. **Every**

promise has been **fulfilled**; **not one has failed.**" *(New International Version)*

Abundantly bless provision

Psalms 132:15, "I will **abundantly** bless her **provision**: I will satisfy her poor with bread."

Food and Drink

Proverbs 3:10, "So shall thy barns be filled with **plenty**, and thy presses shall burst out with new wine."

Seed Increase

Isaiah 30:23, "Then shall he give the rain of thy seed, that thou shalt sow the ground withal; and bread of the increase of the earth, and it shall be fat and **plenteous**: in that day shall thy cattle feed in large pastures."

Multiply, Increase, and no more Reproach

Ezekiel 36:30, "And I will **multiply** the fruit of the tree, and the **increase** of the field, that ye shall receive **no more reproach** of famine among the heathen.

Overtake

Amos 9:13, "Behold, the days come, saith the LORD, that the plowman shall **overtake** the reaper, and the treader of grapes him that soweth seed; and the mountains shall drop sweet wine, and all the hills shall melt."

Possessor of All Things

Zechariah 8:12, "For the seed shall be **prosperous**; the vine shall give her **fruit**, and the ground shall give her **increase**, and the heavens shall give their **dew**; and I will cause the remnant of this people to **possess all these things.**"

Peace

Psalms 85:8, "I will listen to what God the LORD will say; he **promises peace** to his people, his saints-- but let them not return to folly." *(New International Version)*

Psalms 106:12, "Then they believed his **promises** and sang **his praise**." *(New International Version)*

Love

Psalms 119:140, "Your **promises** have been thoroughly tested, and your servant **loves** them." *(New International Version)*

Psalms 145:13, "Your kingdom is an everlasting kingdom, and your dominion endures through all Generations. The LORD is faithful to all his **promises** and **loving** toward all he has made." *(New International Version)*

Meditate

Psalms 119:148, "My eyes stay open through the watches of the night, that I may **meditate** on your **promises**." *(New International Version)*

Chapter Eight

Promise of the Holy Ghost

As Jesus appeared to the disciples in Jerusalem after His resurrection, they saw Him; they touched Him, and ate food with Him. Even though His body wasn't a restored human body like Lazarus's—He was able to appear and disappear. His resurrected body was even more real than before; it was now immortal. This is the kind of body we will be given at the resurrection of the dead according to 1 Corinthians 15:42-50. Just before Jesus vacated the premises, He spoke to the disciples and said:

St. Luke 24:49, "And, behold, I send the promise of my Father upon you: but tarry ye in the city of Jerusalem, until ye be endued with power from on high."

This is the same promise He made that is in the book of Acts:

Acts 1:4, "And, being assembled together with them, commanded them that they should not depart from Jerusalem, but wait for the promise of the Father, which, saith he, ye have heard of me."

Later on the disciples experienced the promise which was told to them:

Acts 2:33, "Therefore being by the right hand of God exalted, and having received of the Father the promise of the Holy Ghost, he hath shed forth this, which ye now see and hear."

The promise didn't stop there! The promise is transgenerational!

Acts 2:39, "For the promise is unto **you**, and to **your children**, and to **all** that are **afar off, even as many as the Lord our God shall call**."

The promise seals us!

Ephesians 1:13, "In whom ye also trusted, after that ye heard the word of truth, the gospel of your salvation: in whom also after that ye believed, ye were **sealed with that holy Spirit of promise**,"

WHY DO WE NEED THIS PROMISE OF THE HOLY GHOST?

Answer: Because **JESUS** said so!

St. John 14:16-17, "And I will pray the Father, and he shall give you another Comforter, that he may abide with you for ever; Even the Spirit of truth; whom the world cannot receive, because it seeth him not, neither knoweth him: but ye know him; for he dwelleth with you, and shall be in you."

Notice the promise is referred to as he. For many years, I have heard preacher refer to the promise or the Holy Ghost as it. But according to the scripture the promise is referred as he. Therefore, we refer to him as he.

As we read John, we see that Jesus prayed that the Father would send another Comforter to abide forever. From the book of Acts, we learn that the Holy Ghost has been given. So, it is not a matter of the Father's *giving* anyone the Holy Ghost. It is a matter of our *receiving* the Holy Ghost. According to John, make no mistake about it, the Holy Ghost is for every believer. As believers, we should desire the working and operating of the power of the Holy Ghost in us everyday of our lives.

WHAT DOES THIS PROMISE HELP US DO?

1. He helps us witness.
2. He helps us remember.
3. He helps us love.
4. He helps us live.
5. He helps us learn.
6. He helps us endure.
7. He helps us work.
8. He helps us give.
9. He helps us change.
10. He helps us speak of Jesus.
11. He helps us see, speak, and do.
12. He helps us operate in the supernatural gifts of the Spirit.

CHAPTER NINE

PROMISE THAT COMES WITH HONORING OUR FATHER AND MOTHER:

Ephesians 6:2, "Honour thy father and mother; which is the first commandment with promise;"

"There is a difference between obeying and honoring. To obey means to do as one is told; to honor means to respect and love. Children are not commanded to disobey God in obeying their parents. Adult children are not asked to be subservient to domineering parents. Children are to obey while under their parents' care, but the responsibility to honor parents is for life."

What is the first commandment with promise?

Exodus 20:12, "Honour thy father and thy mother: that thy days may be long upon the land which the LORD thy God giveth thee."

The promise is to live in peace for generations in the Promised Land. The promise is to have longevity. The promise is to add days to your life. The promise is to live longer which is created by honoring your parents. Isn't it ironic when we honor our parents, God promised to extend life to our live? Isn't it a blessing to know that whatever we are to do on the behalf of God it is extended? In other words, whenever we honor our parents, we receive addition to our lives. We have things added to us because of our level of honoring. Therefore, we can conclude that honor adds to us.

- Honor will add time.
- Honor will add prosperity.
- Honor will add love.
- Honor will add peace.
- Honor will add joy.
- Honor will add friends.
- Honor will add favor.
- Honor will add strength.
- Honor will add promotion.
- Honor will add revelation.
- Honor will add anointing.
- Honor will add increase.

Honor is a magnet that will draw great things to it!

CONCLUSION

In conclusion, as we learn more about God's promises, they are sure and final. So, begin to act upon them and believe them just as they are, without any question. All we have to do is meet the conditions stated in the promise and you will get the benefits. You must not for a moment question what God promises say. His promises do not need to be interpreted by any man. If God said it that settles it! He means what He says, or He would not have given them to you. Remember, it is the enemies' job to cause you to question the promises of God and to wonder if they are true and for you today. Satan knows the very moment you begin to question what God has said, he can tempt you to doubt God's Word. It is true; this is what caused the fall in the beginning, and this is the very first thing you must get victory over if you want to be redeemed from the fall and if you want to get the benefits of the promises. As I close, can I let you in on a little secret? I have good news! Because of Jesus Christ our Lord and Savior, we now have better promises! God reassures us according to Hebrews 8:6, "But now hath he obtained a more excellent ministry, by how much also he is the mediator of a better covenant, which was established upon **better promises**." In the end, we can truly say, "God is good with His promises!"

WHAT OTHERS ARE SAYING ABOUT DR. BEE!

Bishop Bee is one of my spiritual sons. He truly has been a son who has taken the vision of the ministry and the call of God to a higher level. He has worked hard at carrying out "the Great Commission" of Jesus Christ. We are very proud of him and the work that God is doing through his ministry.

Bishop Willie L. Reid, Sr.
Fellowship Bible Baptist Church – Warner Robins, Georgia

I have known Bishop Bee for over 17 years as a fellow pastor and as a devoted friend. He is a man of integrity. He loves the Lord and loves learning the Word. I have worked alongside him, and with the vision. He spoke to me about the vision God gave him and my spirit bore witness with it. The proof of a prophet is that which he speaks comes to pass, and surely what Bishop Bee has spoken did come to pass.

Dr. Dave A. Wilcoxson
New Piney Grove Baptist Church – Macon, Georgia

Bishop Bee and I have been friends for many years and I know him to be a man of excellence. He is a man with a vision, and has a ministry that is making an impact on this region. He is taking the Word to the streets. The people of Christian Fellowship Church are taught to become disciples and are raised up through the Word of God.

Bishop Jeff Poole
New Hope International Church – Warner Robins, Georgia

Bishop Bee is a great man who has a genuine heart for God, and a genuine love for all people. If you spend any time in his presence you will sense his true concern for your well-being spiritually and naturally. As you enter Christian Fellowship Church you will feel the love of God in the atmosphere, and see the love of God shine through the people. It is a ministry that teaches the Word and lives in the Word of God.

Dr. Maurice Watson
Beulahland Bible Church – Macon, Georgia

Bishop Bee is a dedicated and committed man of God. He has always been a faithful son; trustworthy, outgoing and a giver. My wife and I support and love him because of the greatness that he brings out of other people. I have personally seen his church family in action; I know that they love him because of the obedience that's shown to a man of God from his members. He is truly a lovable guy!

Dr. Wesley Bee, Jr.
Christ Church of Universal Love – Valdosta, Georgia

What I admire about Bishop Bee is that he has a spirit of excellence and he makes you feel good about yourself. Under his dynamic leadership, Christian Fellowship Church is destined to do great things for God's Kingdom. He is an awesome teacher, preacher, and a prophet of God. He has a genuine love for God's people by equipping them for the work of the ministry through his bold and practical preaching.

Bishop Larry Manning
New Life Ministries – Valdosta, Georgia

Besides being an anointed proclaimer of the gospel, Bishop Bee has proven himself to be a leader in every sense of the word. He has enhanced the body of Christ and his influence continues beyond our community. As a pastor I appreciate his comradery and thank God for his innovations that help us stretch beyond natural borders. No greater compliment can be given than to say "he is a man of God."

Pastor Melvin Womack
End-Time Harvest Christian Center – Warner Robins, Georgia

Bishop Bee is a world-class leader. His life and servant leadership is the epitome of excellence in ministry. He is committed to the Kingdom's advancement and global expansion. Bishop Bee's covenant partnership with Royal Ambassadors Ministries, Inc. has enabled me to travel to other nations to bring medical supplies, transformational leadership and humanitarian initiatives.

Dr. Keith Rolle
Royal Ambassadors Ministries – San Antonio, Texas

Bishop Bee is a Holy Man of God; a loyal man; a faithful man; a man of integrity; an awesome under-shepherd, a man that loves God and I think most of all, out of these twenty plus years that he has been in ministry there has not been one scandal in his life, financially or with infidelity. "Thank you" Bishop Bee for being an example to the Body of Christ.

Dr. Cornelius Sanders
Revelation Ministries Christian Church – Wichita, Kansas

Because of Bishop Bee's leadership, Christian Fellowship Church is one of the fastest growing ministries in Middle Georgia today. He is making a difference on the behalf of God in the region and in the state. He is definitely a man of excellence and integrity. We have truly been impacted, inspired, and encouraged by his ministry. God is using Bishop Bee to do Kingdom business in the new millennium.

Pastor Kenneth Kirksey
Power House of Faith – Waycross, Georgia

Bishop Bee is very exciting! His ministry is the hottest thing in the Christian world for Middle Georgia. Bishop Harvey Bee is truly a friend. His friendship has proven to be very fruitful. The Christian Fellowship Church, Christian Fellowship Academy, and television broadcast are making an impact on this area for the Kingdom of God.

Pastor David Clarke
Union Grove Missionary Baptist Church – Warner Robins, Georgia

Dr. Harvey Bee is a man with a vision for the Body of Christ. He is a man with the highest level of integrity and he is highly esteemed by his peers as a Pastor, Teacher, and Church

Administrator. He presently serves on the Board of Pastoral Advisors for the Minnesota Graduate School of Theology (MGST). I know this book will be a great value to you– the reader.

Dr. Dave Sigvertsen
President of Minnesota Graduate School of Theology

I have known Bishop Bee since 1991, and have found him to be faithful to his calling, faithful to his family, and a really true friend. He is a dynamic preacher and teacher. His divine purpose is to teach men and women about God, and because of his desire he has been able to stay focused to fulfill that purpose. He is doing great things on the behalf of God.

Pastor Larry Sims, Sr.
Union Tabernacle Baptist Church – Americus, Georgia

I have the pleasure of traveling and ministering to the nations. I can truly say you will never experience a greater anointing than what I experienced at his ministry. The atmosphere is charged with the spirit of expectation. As you enter into the church you will immediately feel the presence of the Lord. Like myself, you will discover that the power of worship and praise is indeed "In the House!"

Psalmist Keith Staten
Tempe, Arizona

ATMOSPHERE MATTERS TO GOD!

ATMOSPHERE DETERMINES WHAT SEEDS GOD WIL
PLANT IN A CERTAIN ENVIRONMENT!

When I entered Dr. Harvey and Veronica's atmosphere,
immediately sensed that this was a place where God's presen
was welcomed and excellence was taught.   I have travel
extensively, and I can say that Christian Fellowship Chur
operates under the anointing of excellence.   Everyone has
attitude of success and treats you with such graciousness. If y
can't succeed under his anointing you will not be able to succe
anywhere else.   I am honored to call Drs. Harvey and Veron
Bee my friend.

Dr. Jerry Grillo
Fogzone Ministries – Hickory North Carolina

BIBLIOGRAPHY:

Holy Bible. *People's Parallel Edition.* King James Version and New Living Translation, Tyndale House Publishers, Inc., 1997.

Dake, Finis Jennings. *The Holy Bible, Dake's Annotated ReferenceBible.* Dake Bible Sales, Inc., 1988.

Holy Bible. *Life Application Bible.* King James Version, Tyndale House Publishers, Inc., 1988.

Bishop Don Meares. *How to Make Your Tithes Start, Stay and Grow.* Seminar, Atlanta, Georgia, 2003.

Reagan Wesley C. *The Highley Commentary.* International Uniform Sunday School Series, Highley Publishing Corporation, 1995-1996.

Thompson, Frank Charles, DD., Ph. D. *The Thompson Chain Reference Bible.* B. B. Kirkbride Bible Company, Inc. 1988.

Dash, Darryl. *Darryl's Sermons.* Website: www.dashhouse.com

QuickVerse. *Bible Reference Collection for Windows.* Parsons Technology, 1995.